The I
Journeys
Around The
World

By S.Z. Ahmed Ph.D

An A.E.R Publication

Library of Congress Catalog Card Number 97-65750

ISBN Number 1-57087-316-X

Production Design by: Robin Ober

Professional Press
Chapel Hill, NC 27515-4371

Manufactured in the United States of America
01 00 99 98 97 96 10 9 8 7 6 5 4 3 2 1

I dedicate this book to all those brave, disciplined and dedicated members of my past expeditions around the world.
We achieved the goals we set in spite of all the hardships encountered to do our research and production of the documentary film.

For-Tes For-Tun-Na Ju-Vat
(Fortune Favors The Bold)

Also By S.Z. Ahmed

Ruwenzori
Twilight Of An Empire (Mughal India)
Twilight Of An Empire (China)
Twilight On The Silk Road (Central Asia)
Twilight On The Caucasus

Contents

Acknowledgment

I would like to acknowledge the friendship of some of the personalities mentioned here:

1. Mr. Shahid Halim and Najma.
2. Mr. Z.U. Ahmed & Rashida.
3. Mr. S. Nasiruddin Ahmed & Zarina And Fatima Nasir
4. Mrs. Bilquis Hyderi & Mr. Sultan Hyadri.
5. Mr. S. Umair Ahmed & Ruhaiya.
6. Group Captain & Begum Khalid Parvez Shah

Also, my old family friend Syed Hamid Ali, with whom I worked to establish the first Airline of Pakistan in 1947. Together, we established the first Air Services from Karachi to Rawalpindi and Peshawar as well as the very first Haj flight to Jedda from Pakistan. I was on this flight as a Traffic Officer for Jedda. Grateful acknowledgments also due specially to Mrs. Susan Ahmed who traveled with me to the "Land Of Lacandones" described in this book. She took pliographs as well as drew sketches appearing in this book. She has also traveled in Europe, Asia, and Africa. Now, she devotes her free time to restoring Antiques. Lastly, I would like to thank Mrs. Alysia Dempsey who provided excellent secretarial services for the manuscripts of this book and previous publications.

Foreword

ne after another lesser known cultures have died and disappeared from this earth, many of which we don't know anything about. While we are trying to preserve wildlife in game preserves, we have a similar but more important duty to record, study and research the few remaining, and lesser known cultures. Not only for ourselves, but for our children, grandchildren, and posterity. Before long our so-called civilization of progress will wipe out these few remaining known cultures.

What is a culture? It is generally agreed that culture is the patterns of behavior rather than behavior. Culture in this sense is not the physical act of doing things but the way in which they are done. Sometimes a man or a woman is quite unaware of his or her own culture. This is a most amazing thing about culture. It is all around us, it shapes our lives, and thoughts, yet we know relatively little about it.

One reason for studying culture is to make the unconscious conscious. To me, as an Anthropologist, a simple cooking pot of a primitive is as much a cultural product as is a Beethoven Sonata. Culture is that complex whole which includes artifacts, beliefs, art and all other habits acquired by a man as a member of a society. All products of human activity is determined by these habits.

In a descriptive sense a culture is a historically derived system of explicit and implicit designs for living which tends to be shared by all or specially designated members of a group. Every human being is born into a world defined by an already existing cultural pattern so that at any point in its history a society can become completely emancipated from its past cultures; this is inconceivable.

In this book I will describe such vanishing cultures and their aspirations. The fundamental problem of mankind is not which specific nation, state or political and economic system is best, it is a matter of discovering that man is more important than any system - and accepting him in all his diversity. Cherishing his different customs, habits, ideas and understanding that is his basic nature to differ creatively and that is where all his ultimate hope lies.

From Arctic to Antarctic there is a tremendous range of climate and life and it is amazing that the same race of people can exist in such extremes of cold and heat. Though a harsh environment, these extremes have intense and dazzling beauty. In the steaming heat of the tropics, nature and her children have remained supreme sovereigns acknowledging no other law other than their own. In the lush green Amazon jungle, light is more beautiful than all the neon signs of the city; the rivers are larger than a hundred highways laid side by side; the desert, whether freezing or torrid is scornful of our air-conditioning.

This is the primitive's home and it controls his mind and way of life. Little is understood of his environment and much is feared. This whole life is a fight against nature and also against the progressive creeping of modern man. What, he asks, is to be left in peace in his own environment. He has no desire to change anyone. He has survived for thousands of years till now, when modern man is threatening his basic existence and his culture.

Through this book I appeal to humanity to preserve and protect the few left over cultures described in this book. The chapters in this book are about those people I have the pleasure of living and working with.

The dazzling aura of rich newcomers from overseas, oil field crews, mineral prospectors, and technicians of all sorts, with their portable air-conditioned villages, bulldozers, helicopters, gadgets, and machines have arrived uninvited in the areas of these vanishing cultures to promote progress. I ask, for whom and at what price.

Introduction

HE INCREDIBLE JOURNEYS AROUND THE WORLD ARE the factual and brief accounts of each of my travels in connection with anthropological research for publication and production of television documentaries which I produced for the networks.

In all these travels the main object was to learn and understand about the people being visited and to provide my observations without the least idea of judging the people. I have never had any inclination to judge or compare them to my culture , way of living, or moral concepts. I believe everyone has a right to live and believe what they think is the best for them to make them happy. I have discovered people can live happily and simply in spite of not having all the modern amenities of our lives.

I tried to keep all the observation and accounts objectively, as I saw and experienced them. This book is for the readers who are interested to know about other people and how they live, or discover by themselves and choose from my account where and what part of the world they want to discover for themselves, or for those people who under the circumstances can not travel but like to read about other people's travel as an armchair traveler.

To lead an Expedition, I found there are problems, such as: selecting the right crew, providing all information available for the area to be traveled; explaining the objectives of the Expedition and all the possible problems that has to be faced and how to solve them. Also, unknown problems may come along which could not be planned and solved in advance, problems of obtaining finances for the Expedition from the donors or financier, and the payment of the money borrowed by marketing the product, such as a book, articles and documentary films, etc. And not the least the matter of security and health of the members of the Expedition and finally obtaining permission and cooperation of the country to be visited and there are many more problems such as supplies, storage and transportation of members and their baggage, etc. I have lived and traveled in Arctic while temperatures were -70°F to 130°F under shade in Sahara Desert in Africa and to this date traveled over 123 countries around the world. Worked with some of the most primitive people in Africa and also the Head hunter in South America but I found that if one was determined to achieve one's goal then it is mind over the body and also one has to pay a price, whatever form it may be. I believe anything that comes easy is not worth to be proud of.

To be a member of an Expedition one has to have a special character that requires discipline, adaptability and determination to achieve your goal. Each member of my Expeditions had those qualities. I hope my readers will enjoy the adventure and incredible journeys from their armchairs.

The desire to travel is not an inborn need in any man or woman, and with some it is a passion and compelling need. I for example I want to discover the remote as well as non-remote areas to travel, see, learn, and experience the life of the other fellow human beings. Plus, as a bonus, I see the different faces of nature and scenic beauties, which could be so different than that place one lives.

I do not understand the apathy of some people who have no desire of seeing some sight which is so very short distance from where they live while people who come from thousands of miles to visit that sight for which they saved perhaps a few years to pay for travel. I give and example. I came from Agra my home town where exists the world's most beautiful monument - called Taj Mahel. I have come across few people in Agra who have never been to Taj Mahel which is walking distance from the city. I am not implying that that kind of person is anyway a less person but the person has no inquisitiveness or desire to know more than what he knows.

Another example I know a person who served in the military and had an opportunity to travel free of charge anywhere in the world by AirForce planes going to the countries embassies around the world, but he never left his country except to serve in the war on a ship. The result, he is totally unaware of the world and the people who live there, their culture, religion, and language. He does not know anything about anyone other than his own while he has this opportunity to discover his fellow beings. He has a large collection of books which he collects to show off to the visitors. He has no conversation about the world we live in. It is pathetic and he is a teacher by profession and knows so little about the world he lives in.

The whole object of this book is not to teach or preach but to make the readers understand that there is no such thing as a standard of my kind from which we can judge people. Each society has his own character and his own natural environment in which they have to survive. There is no such thing as one person is better than the other. A person born in the great Sahara desert of Africa or Arctic of Canada is not inferior to those who are born in the suburbs of Boston or Vienna, or Tokyo. We are all different and live, or have to live under different circumstances therefore, we are not superior or inferior. We try to fit the best way we know to survive to given circumstances. We are not even born equal. This is a myth we are told. I believe each person is born differently to perform a certain task which they do well and perhaps better than others; such as a person who may be a first class tailor and another a first class chemist. None is superior or inferior but, they are also not equal in intelligence. Both perform a very important service to the society in their own way but they are not born equal, no matter what political slogans may say. This book will take you to far and distant places and give you a glimpse of various cultures and societies where I traveled, some are still to be found and some have vanished forever.

I have seen in Kunming in China a very old lady walking in the street with tiny bound feet only about 4" long. A sign of beauty in Imperial China of 19th Century, or in Ubangi Sharie in Central Africa is the upper and lower lips with huge plates in the center are the Ubangi tribes sign of beauty. I have seen enlarged earlobes of certain Amazon tribes in Brazil, a sign of beauty. One may say in Western or modern society how ugly, but don't forget, "Beauty is in the eyes of the beholder."

This book will take you to the places some people dream about and travel agents don't advertise about. It is very exciting, about a year before I plan to leave I try to read as many books as I can find on that area and then make notes on what I can not find in the books, that I have to find when I am there to complete the research. In most of the cases when I was on the location the most common question asked from me was why I am here? What am I going to do here? I have to give them the simple answer I want to know and know all about you and that is why I am here.

The Land Of The Amazon

NTOMOLOGISTS DIVIDE UP THE WORD "AMAZON" AS "A" - without, and "mazos"- breast, meaning without a breast. This is based on the legend, unsubstantiated, of the martial women who sacrificed the natural functions of their sex. The loss of the right breast was supposed to make drawing a bowstring easier. Another explanation derives from the words "hamo" - bound, and "zona" - a belt. The zona which they wore was also the protection of their virginity, pledged by sacred oath.

The fame of the riches of the Indian tribe Manao, with its capital Manaos, on the River Amazon, full of gold, silver and precious stones, reached Europe and spread like wildfire. El Dorado became a household word. Sir Walter Raleigh in 1617 set out on an expedition of discovery. He failed in his mission, owing to many brushes with the Spaniards and finally returned to England. He was later executed for his failure by his ungrateful monarch. Whatever past legends may tell, and whether they are based on fact or fiction, I have no doubts about the actual existence of the Amazonas I visited.

The Amazon, that great and mighty river, flows through three countries of South America - Peru, Columbia, and Brazil. The whole area is known as Amazonas. It is like a tropical garden - a blaze of gorgeous color and a profusion of strange and exquisite shapes. Everything is on a vast scale, with immense jungles and rivers whose details are lost in the expanse. There are very few tracks; most thoroughfares are waterways. There is an abundance of wildlife, but the greatest danger tot he traveler is from falling trees. A sudden crack, a startling noise in the all-pervading stillness, will give warning of an impending fall. It may be in the distance or it may be right beside you. You may be a sudden victim. Noises can be deceptive.

The light of glow worms and fireflies at night is so brilliant that it is possible, in a moment of forgetfulness, to mistake them for the distant light of a native hut. The stillness and quiet of the forest is a very real thing. I have journeyed for a whole day in a canoe and never seen a human being. Sometimes the vibrant quietness will suddenly be broken by a shrill scream. Some creature has reached the end of his journey.

From sunset to sunset is the noisiest time in these jungles, when monkey loudly discuss their next day's program and toucans and muti-colored parrots cannot settle their differences peaceably. That is the time when the steaming jungle is most alive and most vociferous. Picture all this, and try to understand the people of the Amazonas. The space at my disposal is so restricted that I will describe very briefly a life cycle of a tribe call Yahua, or Yagua, a native of Amazonas.

Certain of the Yagua customs and habits reveal the influence of the Incas of Peru. The people are tall with tawny yellow complexions and lighter-colored hair than other Indians. They have a dozen or so clans, named after different animals or cereals, such as the Cat Clan or the Cotton Clan. Their clothes are made from palm tree fiber, *mairota flexuosa*. Often the garment is dyed a rusty red color with achote. The ceremonial masks are also dyed the same color. The men wear a fiber band around their head and also one around the base of the neck. Women wear the neck band only, and its length is greater than the men's, extending to the lower line of the breasts.

A single community lives in one single house that is made of palm leaves and a framework of wooden poles. There is one door and a few windows, with a palm lead curtain to be used against adverse weather. In the center of the hut is a communal fireplace, but most of the cooking is done out of doors.

The main occupation of the men is hunting and occasionally fishing. They eat all animals except pets and reptiles, like the Boa. Most of the hunting is done by blow-gun and poisoned arrows, which are silent and effective. They also use straps. I remember watching them fish. They used Barbasco poison, crushing the roots into a pulp and then throwing it into a damned channel. After a short time the poison dissolves in the water, and the stupefied fish float on their bellies to the surface.

Apart from meat and fish their diet includes bananas, sweet potatoes, papaya, and palm kernels. Their favorite drink is Massoto, fermented drink made from manioc. The method of preparation is interesting. The elderly women of the clan chew the manioc to induce fermentation and when it is well chewed, spit it into an earthenware pot, where it is left to ferment.

Childbirth is simple and primitive, like all other things. Inside the house against the walls, two pieces of wood or two logs are placed about a foot apart, on a mattress of palm leaves. During labor the woman sits on these two pieces of wood and holds onto the wall of the hut. She is supported in the sitting position from behind by women attendants and the baby drops onto the mattress below. After the birth, baby and mother go to the nearest stream to bathe. The father is told the news and he retires to rest for two to three days. He does no work, is fed in his hammock, and can eat or drink anything except fish or fowl. The mother's routine of chores goes on without a break after the birth of the baby.

At the age of puberty the girls are moved to a separate hut and at the first sign of menstruation are put on a diet by the elderly women. After about ten days they are ceremoniously bathed in the stream with aromatic plants and then return to their normal life. When the boys arrive at that age they are sometimes circumcised. Sex relations before marriage are common and take place at the early age of twelve or thirteen. The average marriage age for a girl is twelve, for a boy fourteen. Girls generally marry when their breasts start to be prominent and boys when they can support themselves by hunting. There are no initiation ceremonies such as I have seen in tropical Africa during my travels in the Sudan, the Congo, and other parts.

When a boy and girl decide to marry, the boy approaches the girl's parents to ask permission. If it is granted, the girl's parents arrange a wedding feast and the entire clan of the groom is invited. The guests arrive on the day with their own food and drink, as well as their own cooking pots. First comes a round of Massoto, and then the food which is shared from a central place. It is followed by dances of men with men and women with women. The whole program continues until night draws in and then everyone retires to the host's house - the family to their hammocks, the guest to the floor. After the wedding there follows a period of service performed free by the groom for his father-in-law as a bride-price. The groom stays at his bride's home for approximately six months and helps his father-in-law with hunting and fishing and other tasks. Then, on the termination of the agreed period, he moves with his bride to his own community.

The Yagua bury their dead in a sitting position with all their clothes on. The hammocks of the house are also wrapped around his body, which is buried under the floor of the house. The Yagua have a great respect for privacy. They show it in an unusual custom which is very strictly observed. If a man, woman or child lies down facing the wall of the hut, he or she cannot be disturbed. No one can even speak to them, since they are not "at home" and so cannot hear.

The reason for the Yagua's persistently primitive state is the little or non-existent contact with people outside the tribe. This is due to the difficult terrain and to the lack of means of communication. They restrict their movements to their own known domains. This great child of nature goes in terror of everything, yet he is very brave. Death which he deals so valiantly he does not fear to meet. He fears the unknown which he cannot describe, the unknown which blows the howling wind, the long dark shawdows, thundery storms and what to follow after death?

The Land Of The Chimborazo

CUADOR, FOR MORE THAN FOUR CENTURIES, HAS attracted many of the world's greatest explorers, geographers, naturalists, and scientists and has been the source of vital discoveries of benefit to mankind. It was in Ecuador that the true shape of the earth was established by the eminent French mathematician Charles de la Condamine, who in 1735 headed the first scientific expedition to South America. From its headquarters in Quito, which this expedition measured an arc of the meridian at the equator, the measurement upon which the metric system was based. In 1797 Alexander von Humboldt, the great German explorer and geographer, visited Ecuador. He discovered the Antarctic current which bathes the Pacific Coast as far north as Ecuador's Cape Pasado; the current was later named after him.

Few if any countries in the world posses as many varieties of native plants and trees as Ecuador, including rare species of industrial and medicinal value. Mankind has derived incalculable benefits, for example, from Ecuador's quina tree, source of quinine; it later received the name cinchona, derived from that of the Countess of Chinchon, the wife of a Spanish viceroy of Peru who, in 1631, was cured of malaria by a native remedy made of the bark of the quina tree when she fell ill en route to Quito. More the forests of the Loja and Bolivar Provinces the seeds and plants which were the beginning of the great cinchona plantations of India and Ceylon.

The history of Ecuador is a long and romantic one, interspersed with periods of peaceful progress and violent struggle. By 1526 the Inca Huayna Capac had consolidated his conquest and after dividing the kingdom between his two sons, Huascar and Atahualpa, he retired in ill health to his sumptuous palace at Tomebamba. It was here that he received word that strange white folk in a large craft had been seen off the coast. The white strangers were Spaniards who landed on the shore of Ecuador on the first trip of exploration along the west coast. Francisco Pizarro led the next two expeditions from his base in Panama.

After exploring the coast and seizing the treasures at Atacames, Pizarro returned to Spain in 1528 convinced that he had discovered a rich kingdom. It was about this time that Huayna Capac died, thus giving ride to the fratricidal wars between the half brothers Huascar and Atahualpa for control of the Inca Empire. Atahualpa defeated Huascar and became master of Cuzco as well as Quito, but the struggle had weakened the Inca force to such an extent that when Pizarro returned several years later and began the conquest of the Inca Empire, he encountered little resistance. The Indians, moreover, regarded the Spaniards as curiosities rather than conquerors, not only because of their white skins, but also because of their horses - the first ever seen in South America. They believed that the invaders were powerless when dismounted and therefore offered little resistance to their attacks.

The Inca Atahualpa, taken by surprise at his mountain retreat in Cajamarca, some 500 miles south of Quito on the Camino Real, was captured in 1532 and held prisoner while his subjects filled a room full of gold and another of silver to fulfill the terms of his ransom. Not content with this vast treasure, Pizarro had Atahualpa put to death, thus inaugurating a long period of ruthless warfare against the native population. Although the last of the Incas was dead, Quito was not subdued until Pizarro dispatched Sebastian de Benalcaar to take possession of the northern kingdom before a rival Spanish conquistador could do so. Benalcazar carried out the mandate and founded San Francisco de Quito on December 6, 1534, on the site of the ancient Quito capital. Gonzalo Pizarro, a brother of Francisco, was named governor of the colony in 1540. The colonial periods of Ecuador's history covered almost three centuries, from the fall of the Inca Empire to the winning of independence from Spain in 1822.

The subjugation of the native population was followed by rivalries and civil strife of such intensity and violence among the conquerors that both Francisco Pizarro and his partner Diego do Almagro were murdered before the end of 1541 in Peru. The insatiable greed of their followers for gold and treasures was further whetted by tales told to them by the Indians of the land of El Dorado (the Gilded Man) and of a region rich in cinnamon and spices.

In search of these, Gonzalo Pizarro organized an expedition in Quito in 1541 which resulted in the discovery of the Amazon River the following year. In a fantastic trek, the expedition crossed the Andes and built a brigantine on the Coc River to continue explorations. Orellana, who was sent ahead in the ship to find and bring back food, swept into the night Napo

River and continued into the Amazon, which he followed down its 3,990-mile course into the Atlantic Orellana found neither the land of cinnamon nor that of the "gilded man," his discovery of the great river brought him rich rewards at the court of Spain.

Exploration, colonization, and the implanting of Spanish civilization went forward. The first schools were established by the religious order of the Catholic Church, whose selfless missionaries sought to bring peace tot he strife-torn colony. Until 1830, the native population remained in a service state under the encomienda system, encomendero. Quito, capital of the colony, grew and prospered. Its request to be made a royal audiencia was granted by Spain in 1563. Although primarily a superior court of justice, the Royal Audiencia of Quito also exercised political and military functions. Its jurisdiction extended beyond the present limits of modern Ecuador; it was responsible to the Viceroyalty of Peru, of which it formed a part until 1718, and thereafter to the Viceroyalty of Peru, of which it formed a part until 1718, and thereafter to the Viceroyalty of New Grenada with its seat in Bogota. Later the colony was elevated to the rank of a presidency.

Modern Ecuador has a rich and varied cultural heritage derived from prehistoric Indian civilizations. The art and architecture of Spain's Golden Age Transplanted to the colony in the seventeenth century, and the literary and artistic achievements of the colonial and republican periods. Today, the nation's cultural tradition is carried on by a new generation of creative artists and writers, educators and scientists.

From Indian burial mounds and ruins in the Andean highlands and along the coast, archaeologist have uncovered pottery, jewellery, and stone objects which resemble the culture of pre-Inca fortresses and temples. The most impressive Ecuadorean example of stone masonry, for which the Incas were famous, is the ruin of the citadel of Incapirca on the cold Andean plateau of Canar Province. In the villages of Chardeleg and Sigsig, not for from Cuencia, archaelogists have uncovered golden crown and breastplates and gold-banded weapons. Near La Tola in the north, golden artifacts, molded figurines, bowls, stone axes, and other relics have been uncovered in burial mounds, or tolas, left by a prehistoric Indian civilization which attained a high degree of culture.

Ecuador's present-day population of more than 10,600,000 inhabitants represents a rich mosaic of different racial and cultural elements, composed principally of white population and a substantial mesizo class, Ecuador has some of the most interesting Indian tribes and communities of South America - the resourceful Otavalas of the Andean highlands who excel in arts and crafts, the docile Colorados of the western jungle who are diminshing in number, the primitive Jivaras of the isolated Oriente, and the Aucas, who are as much a mystery to other Ecuadoreans as they are to the outside world.

The large black population of the city of Esmaraldas is descended from slaves who, in the sixteenth century, successfully fought for their freedom against both Indians and whites and created a small independent empire under the leadership of two men who escaped from a slave ship in 1533.

The backbone of the country is formed by two parallel ranges of the Andes - the Cordillera Oriental on the eastern range, and the Cordillera Occidental, on the western range, which runs from north to south through the center of the country for a distance of about 500 miles. The two cordilleras divide the country lowlands bordering the Pacific Ocean; the inter-Andean or highland section called the Sierra; and the Oriente, or eastern lowlands having a tropical climate and heavy rainfall.

Some parts of the Oriente are a green hell, inaccessible tot he tourist. After the tropical sun the shade seems like darkness, but offers no relief from the heat. If anything, it seems hotter in the shade as sweat rolls from one's face and one's shirt clings tot he back. Mosquitos, wasps and insects play hell with exposed parts of the body.

Man is dwarfed in the thick, lush vegetation of plants, shrubs and creepers, and the ground is covered by thick layers of damp and rotting plants and leaves. Out of this rich chaos grow trees, some as high as two hundred feet. Their branches are festooned with creepers and their fallen leaves cover the ground like a wet carpet. The forest is full of noises of things that crawl, leap, run and climb, chatter and shriek. Occasionally, not too far off one can hear the sounds of wild boar fighting for survival. The blossoms are surrounded by bees, brilliant blue, red, and multi-colored butterflies, and on some of the trees fruits are eaten by vivid birds and black furry monkeys during the endless summer, with rain and nightfall the only varying themes.

The foliage of the forest canopy maintains an everlasting shade from the tropical sun, which would otherwise have allowed the torrential rain to wash away the fertile woody stem of the lianas creep five or six hundred feet, supporting themselves on the trees, spreading up and down.

In the armpits of many giant trees, lodged in the crevices, are orchids and other flowers, ferns, and mosses of all descriptions, size and color. Some roots hang in the humid air to suck its moisture. It is the greenhouse of the world, savage with life. Millions of worms and insects eat the fallen trees and fungi on the sweaty floor of the forest. In the shade there is the chaos of the vegetation, alive and dead, things fallen and growing, and a great tumult of voices of birds, toucans, monkeys, and parrots shrieking recognizably close at hand, but invisible.

In this green hell live the brave warriors, the "Aucas," who refuse to be subdued and are still children of nature. They love their privacy and expect others to respect it. They do not fear death but the unknown, that which they cannot describe, which could be modern civilization or the howling wind, the long, dark shadows, thundry tropical storms, and what road the soul will take after death.

Beside the Aucas live their neighbors the "Cofanes," the gentle people of the Oriente and other primitive and semi-.primitive tribes of the Amazon Basin with dozens of dozens of clans. Their clothes are made from palm tree fiber, called *Mauritia Flexuosa* Often the garments of the men and women's shirts are dyed with achote to form a rusty red color. A single family lives in one single house that is made of palm leaves and a framework of wooden poles. There is one door and a few windows, with a palm curtain to be used against adverse weather. In the center or to one side of the hut is a fireplace.

Hammocks are used for sleeping.

The main occupation of the men is hunting and fishing and some agriculture. They eat all animals except pets and reptiles, like the Boa. Most of the hunting is done by blow gun and poisoned arrows, which are silent and effective. They also use traps. Their favorite drink is Chicha The method of preparation is interesting. The elderly women of the household chew the manioc to induce fermentation and when it is well chewed, spit it into an earthenware pot, where it is left to ferment.

The childbirth of some of the tribes is simple, like all other things. Inside the house against the walls, two pieces of wood or two logs are placed about a foot apart, on a mattress of palm leaves. During labor the woman sits on these two pieces of wood and holds on to the wall of the hut. She is supported in the sitting position from behind by women attendants and the baby drops onto the mattress below. After the birth, baby and mother go to the nearest stream to bathe. Then they return to the hut to resume normal life.

At the age of puberty the girls are moved to a separate hut and at the first sign of menstruation are put on a diet by the elderly women. After about ten days they are ceremoniously bathed in the stream with aromatic plants and then return to their normal life. Sex relations before marriage are common and take place at the early age of twelve or thirteen.

The primitives of this area bury their dead in a sitting position with all their clothes on. The personal hammock of the dead person and his utensils are buried along with him.

These people are able to live in a primitive state because there is little or no contact with people outside the tribe.

This is due to the difficult terrain and to the lack of means of communication. They restrict their movements to their own known domain.

Ecuador is one of the few countries of South America so rich in history, culture and natural beauty. Quito is a capital with modern buildings, beautiful villas, etc. One can walk down San Francisco church and feel transported to the 18th century. Ecuador is a country with rising prosperity and stability, the Switzerland of South America. It is a paradise, yet few know about it despite the modern means of transport available. How little we know about the places on our own planet.

The Land Of The High Atlas

RAVELING THROUGH THE HIGH ATLAS COUNTRY OF Morocco can never be boring, not only because of the varied landscapes but also because of the thousand details of the life of the mountain people.

The traveler is captivated by the sight of the men, bareheaded and shaven, wrapped up in a long cloak of grey wool, "the Azenagh" or wearing the "aknif," which is strangely decorated with a red motif in the back, and the women cleverly draped in vermilion wool. One is surprised imaging the tough and monotonous existence of the mountain dwellers in the wild or graceful surroundings in which they are to be seen.

It is a charming sight to see the leaping waters and the green fields damp with dew when one wakes on a magical morning after the veils of night have disappeared. Two women are climbing an embankment. Each one carries a basket on her head. They stop and put down their burdens. One stands on tip-toe in her hare feet to -reach the lower branches of a walnut tree. The other bends down to the grass to pick up the leaves sent down by her companion with her arms raised, the body outstretches under the rough wool held by silver fibulas.

They seem to be going through an ancient rite, like garden divinities hailed by Virgil or Horace. But let not these poetic thoughts mask reality. The mountain girl of the High Atlas is often beautiful but rarely pretty. Some superb types are to be seen occasionally, with sculptural lines and lissome limbs. But this beauty scarcely lasts; heavy work and painful births soon get the better of them.

Or the traveler who goes off the beaten track may see a delicious little idyll, at midday, not far from an Ait Telti village, in a well hidden spot where a group of young girls standing in the water take a bath by pouring water on themselves with an earthenware pot. They bathe with such natural grace. They throw the water so adroitly that two or three aspersions are enough to wet all their body. From time to time an unrepressed laugh peals out to be stopped by the frightened looks of the others. The bath may continue without prudery or without any idea of indecency. One would not dare disturb such a fresh picture.

In the High Imdghas, three silent little shepherds roast some corn cobs on a fire, and the thin column of blue smoke rises straight in the russet shadows of the mountain. A song also rises skyward. In a narrow plot of barley close to the torrent, I can see among the golden ears a woman in a vermillion tunic squatting down with her sickle, singing.

It is like Wordsworth's "Solitary Reaper," whose melancholy song follows me as I go along the valley: "Will no one tell me what she sings?"

Perhaps the plaintive numbers flow
For old and happy far off things
And battles long ago.
Or is it some more humble lay
Familiar matter of today,
Some natural sorrow, loss or pain
That has been and may be again?

Annemiter is one of the prettiest of the High Atlas villages with its white, pink, yellow, or brown houses strung out in a semicircle between the bare mountains and the gardens planted with thick fig trees. In single file about 30 mountain men dressed in their curious black and white striped robes can be seen looking like old time convicts.

At a signal they all lift their "aguelzim," the triangular iron hoe, and with a grunt, they all bring it down together to break the soil in perfect unison. One of the men introduces a song. Then comes another phrase which the others repeat while he remains silent. The choir-like singing continues. Slowly the rhythm gets faster, and the workers increase the tempo with their hoes. The deeply turned soil seems to writhe under their rhythmically advancing feet. The sods thrown behind send up a cloud of golden dust. And then doubtless at a signal, the tools stop above their heads for an instant. A long cry is heard which stops suddenly as the heavily breathing and sweating men drive the shiny blades of the hoes into the ground.

After a few moment's rest, the work starts again and with it, the song. The owners of the land who have the workers today bring the meal before midday; it is substantial, usually made of barley couscous, meat, skimmed milk and mint tea. When the sun gets hot the workers go for a siesta in the shadow of the trees.

Aeoli sleeps at the top of the silver branches. Philomen dreams in the semi- darkness of the fig tress and trills her song sent back by Echo, who watches constantly down the valley. The kestrel screeches as it flies low over the meandering stream. The crow suffocating in the hot air caws in the foliage braised by the noOnday sun. The birds of prey reply as they wheel out over the scattered flocks on the russet slopes devoured by the sun at its zenith.

Later, the drowsy countryside comes out of its torpor as the clink of the tools and the bucolic songs start again. The same scenes of communal labor can be met with in other valleys where the mountain dwellers put into practice the precept "one for all and all for one." When the plowing season comes, the villagers cast lots with small stones or twigs to decide which part of their region will be worked first. Without any distinction as to the proprietor, all join in the job. Two or three men from each family participate, according to size, and they dig all the land, moving from plot to plot until the whole village's soil is turned. These rustic scenes, the men and the things of the land, have always gripped me.

I know of nothing so pleasing to the eye as the valley with blue slopes, with a field of dark green clover or young maize in which the working women make splashes of orange, scarlet, and vermilion with their tunics.

Forty years ago I contacted the people of the eastern High Atlas who saw a foreigner for the first time. When their first fears had gone, the mountain women with their tresses held by silver rings in the way of Etruscan women were most curious and went so far as to touch my clothes and shoes.

Dear Chleuhs of unknown lands! They welcomed me wherever I wandered in their country, and their last words as I left were those of a Rudyard Kipling hero, "We have talked with open hearts and eaten from the same dish, for us you have been a brother..."

I was often just as amazed as they were. Not a day passed without exciting discoveries like the curious agrarian rites which are survivals of pagan cults that disappeared centuries ago. Two examples are enough to underline the strange and mysterious character of proprietary rites, a list of which would be tedious.

To stop the torrential rains that threaten harvests, the High Atlas mountain dweller pretends to plow a corner of a field with a dog and a cat harnessed to a stick that represents the plowshare. To make it rain when the season has been dry, young girls dressed in their best clothes take a stroll through the crops with a kind of doll they call "Taghonja," (literally the spoon). Some of the girls sing "Taghonja! What is your husband's name?" and the others reply "My husband is called Ounzari!" (the rain).

Living out in the open in the limpid purity of silvered sunlight, far from the agitation below, the mountain people have adopted simple mores and have honest hearts. The population of the remote villages show very clearly some of the most salient features of their race. It is thought and too often said that the mountain people are hard. The kind of life imposed on them by hard daily labor is certainly not conducive to the refinements that rapidly lead to decadence among civilized peoples. They are not overly sensitive, but on occasion they display virility and they are not ungenerous.

They have calm courage and tranquil audacity born of the contact with hostile nature and ever-vigilant enemies which have molded their hard-cast character. One senses that none of them wish to be otherwise, none desire to change their fortunes, and yet calm and contentment are written on their faces. It is in impenetrable race and we are a long way from understanding people so far removed from our western conceptions. But their calm and contentment are often circumstantial and deceptive, for misfortunes are not lacking, nor are the objects of discontent. But in the High Atlas, as anywhere, there is deep down in the heart of each man a ray of hope.

Among the memories that mark my journeys through the Atlas mountains, there are several I like to relay because they are so characteristic of the primitive Chleuh, his naive and childlike char, at once suspicious and spontaneous, and often motivated by the noblest sentiments.

One day I was going up the Tassaout Valley, when near the village of Tallemt I found a veritable field of watercress growing along a river. Having been living on dried vegetables for months, I was delighted to eat the fresh greenery. But I was being watched by two laborers who stopped their plow.

One of them shouted "Zrit! Zrit! Roumi-ad aich touga zound tafounast!" In other words, "Look at the foreigner who is eating the grass like a cow!" It was so unexpected and the tone so funny that I burst out laughing. The two Chleuhs did the same and came running down the hill. I managed to convince them that watercress had virtues and after a lot of hesitation, they started to eat the grass...like cows!

Once in the fine forest of the Ait Brahim I asked directions of an old shepherd. His reply was as follows: "Keep walking! Follow the paths which always leads somewhere, and if you leave the path, do you think there will be no more ground?" I could not help thinking that

Homer's wandering heroes must have often heard answers like that.

Going up the Tasselmt stream, I stopped for the night near a spring and lit my fire. Two women came by, bent under heavy faggots of wood. A few moments later a jovial but somewhat irritated Chleuh came to kick my burning twigs all over the place. Before I could object, he took my things on his shoulder and shouted, "You are a man who wants to cover us with shame! Do you think you can stay here, two rifle shots' distance from our village, like a leper? Praise be to God, there is a lighted hearth in our house and we have the wherewithal to welcome you properly. Be welcome!"

How could one be impervious to such simple words full of high nobility and such rough but touching gestures?

One evening after spending days traveling across the empty wastes of the Adrar n'Ououchene, I arrived at the Tizi n'Laaz, which means "The pass of hunger," a name whiich is completely justified, because far hundreds of yards the pass is a nightmare chaos of rocks like a gigantic quarry. I went down along the way on the steep Azourki mountain behind which the sun had already set, and I arrived at the Asemouk fort in the middle of the night. The fort was a modest square of masonry enclosing miserable shelters where three or four mokhazni guards were stationed to guard the pass.

I knocked on the iron door, and a voice from a slit in the wall, where I could see a glinting rifle in -the moonlight, said "Who goes there?" "A weary and thirsty man just come from the Tizi n'Laaz. You have water and fire and I have the necessary items to make tea that we shall drink together..."

"Only jackals and bandits are abroad on the trails at midnight; only the devil would come from Tizi n'Laaz at this hour." A musket barrel was poked out of the gate. A brutal and imperative voice told him to go away. Could the traveler say he was a foreigner? He would not be believed, wearing-a long chleuh cloak, he looked like a Moroccan to the guards, and so he had to continue with the pretence.

"How many are you?" asked a voice.

"Two," I replied, I thought this would seem less bizarre in such a strange and risky country. The gate was pushed ajar and two muskets were poked out. Then a lantern held at arm's length lit up the visitor's face. A foreigner! Surprised and disturbed, the mokhaznis continued on the defensive.

"You said there were two of you. Where is your companion?" The time had come to win them over and reassure them. Laughing, the foreigner shook the guard by the shoulder and said, "I count for two people, myself with God's blessing!"

The mokhaznis said "The night is dark, but your words chase the shadows away! Whoever comes down from Tizi n'Laaz in the middle of the night and alone, under the protection of God, is worth two men!"

The guards showered all kinds of attention on me. They told stories and drank tea until dawn. A simple joke at the right time had been enough to win the confidence of the mountain men.

I continued on his way and the warm parting handshakes of my hosts expressed-all their esteem for a friendship as solid as the "azazar" plant whose roots cling to the beetling rock for centuries. It is true that a simple anecdote is more eloquent than expert studies.

The Land of The Veiled Men

UAREGS ARE KNOWN AS "THE PEOPLE OF THE VEIL" OR in their language KelTagilmus. They are the knights and nobles of the desert My arrival in a Tuareg camp in the Western Sahara caused a certain amount of excitement, but the novelty soon wore and when routine life was resumed I was able to observe the customs and habits of these people.

My guide and friend during my stay at the camp was Mohammad. He was an ideal specimen of a Tuareg, being six feet five inches tall, slight build, with a heavy dark beard and mustache. He had a domed forehead, heavy eyebrow bones and the characteristic Libyan indentation between the forehead and root of the nose, which from that point is straight to the flat extremity. His nostrils were moderately thin and lips were fine. There was an indentation between the lower lip and chin, which was very pointed. The cheek bones were prominent but not very high; the outline of the face running straight down to the chin. The ears were small, thin and flat. The profile is no doubt prozhinous. His hands and ankles were as slender as those of a woman; his body and waist were also slender, and as is the case among all Tuareg, there was no superficial muscle development. Generally Tuareg have grey or light brown eyes and jet black hair, which is not crinkled unless their blood is mixed with Negro. I have seen fair skinned Tuaregs which are a pure breed but the vast majority are dark skinned. All the Oalad.E-Yahya I met were dark skinned with straight hair. Part of this darkness of skin is due to the indigo-dyed clothes they use. The extreme shortage of water makes it impossible to wash frequently and the stain of the indigo dye colors the skin, protecting it from the sun's strong rays.

The principal characteristic of the Tuareg is the beauty and grace of their bodies. I never came across a fat Tuareg. They walk like Princes of the Earth in their flowing robes. These black robes are called Takatkat, under which they wear Takirbai, a type of trouser made of white cotton. Their sandals are made of camel hide. The Tuareg is never without his veil. Night and day, sleeping, eating, traveling or fighting, the veil is never removed.

Many theories have been advanced to explain the wearing of this veil. Some think it is a protection against sand and wind, and others think it is a disguise such as those worn by bandits. There is also a theory that the veil was handed down from the period when the Negro Empires swept over the Sahara from the south. The Tuareg, being in the minority, put on the black veil in order to pass as Negroes and thus escape death. The effect of seeing the tall, veiled silent men is quite inspiring and also somewhat frightening. The dark blue and black veils lend an air of mystery and I always felt that they created an atmosphere of strong animosity. Whatever the origin of the veil, it is certain that it has been a great protection to Tuareg raiders, for when masked they are unrecognizable and have again and again escaped punishment because no accuser could point his finger at any one of them and be certain of correct identification. Such raiding parties will not kill unless they are attacked. During a raid women and children are not touched. Houses and property are not destroyed or burned. Usually camels and livestock are captured and taken away.

The Tuareg woman does not wear a veil, she does not travel the desert and spends most of her life is spent in or around the tent She wears a long piece of indigo cloth rolled round her body like a skirt and tucked in at the waist. Over her shoulder is a garment which resembles a sleeveless coat. Emancipation of women, which is a very modern concept in the Western World, has been practiced among the Tuaregs for centuries. Their women hold positions and prerogatives not yet achieved by their sisters in many of the Western countries which we term "civilized." According to Islamic doctrine, a Tuareg woman may own property in her own name, and she may continue to do so after marrying without interference from her husband, who has no rights over her possessions whatsoever. The Tuareg woman can sit in the Tribal Council Often, women have become rulers of the village, and on occasions women have led punitive expeditions, fighting better than the men. The richer women are generally fat, but when the women do not run to fat, they age with great beauty. Nearly all the old women looked like typical aristocrats and were conscious of their breeding. The Tuareg women have an unfailing sense of humor and are constantly cheerful in spite of their tough life.

The children of the Tuareg, especially the little girls, are adorable. They are fairer-than their parents, largely because I think they wash more often than their elders. Up to the age of seven or eight the children wear no clothes at all, summer or winter, indoors or outdoors.

Perhaps to keep off the flies, they wear a rag when sleeping. Small boys have their hair cropped close, except for a crest along the top of the head, and little girls have long hair. Tuareg children are well behaved, have perfect manners, and are most unselfish. I found that if I gave sweets or coins to a child, he would offer it to his parents and if they refused, would then offer it to his companions. Only if no one accepted it, and only then, did it belong to him. As the boys grow they accept domestic duties and work on the camp. The feed the camels on the road, carry water for their elders to drink, and graze the camels. So before they mature, they are already responsible and have learned to respect their elders; in fact, they have definite roles within the community.

My first meal at a Tuareg camp consisted of fresh dates and newly-made cheese known as *tikammar*, which was presented to me by the Chief of the Tuaregs. Later I learned more about their diet and how they prepare their food.

The staple diet is milk and cheese. Tuaregs make their cheese from goat or camel's milk. The curds are pressed in matting made of palm fronds and formed into cakes which are about five inches square by one inch thick. The fresh cheese is pure white. It is soft, but at the same time crisp, and it is delicious with dates or any form of food. It has no sour or cheesy flavor, although when dried it is yellow and hard, and if used when stale, it requires soaking and has a rather unpleasant smell. The Tuaregs make butter by churning the milk in a goat's skin shaped like a milk bottle.

Flour is made from powdered millet and mixed with water and dry powdered cheese. The dry cheese gives it a sour taste which one gets used to and after a while it becomes refreshing if one is thirsty. They also bake cakes made from millet flour. Meat is seldom eaten, for it is a luxury, but when an animal is slaughtered and divided up, the Tuaregs do not know how to roast or fry. They stew their meat in a pot with vegetables or they add the meat to a form of porridge which is cooked in water or sometimes in oil. If there is a surplus of meat, it is preserved by soaking it in brine after which it is strung on cords and dried in the sun. In an emergency, Tuaregs collect seeds of various grasses and grind them, especially a grass called Afora and a prickly burr grass. The former Is a tall grass with stems of such strength that when dried they are used for making mats, etc. Dates are eaten fresh, or are preserved by soaking them for a short time in boiling water and pressing them into airtight Leather receptacles which are then sewn up. Some Tuaregs dry their dates and string them together after removing the stones.

The food is generally cooked in pear-shaped earthenware pots. These are plain with a lip or rim around the mouth which is bound with a cord to prevent cracking. The food is cooked by the women, or while on the marches, by the youngest member of the party. The indigenous and primitive fashion is to grind grain on the rudimentary saddle stone quern, a form which has been presumably unchanged since prehistoric times. A large flat stone is placed on the ground and the person grinding millet or wheat kneels by it with a basket under the opposite lip of the stone to catch the four as it is made. The wheat or other grain is poured onto the flat stone and crushed by rubbing it with a saddle stone or rounded pebble about the size of a grapefruit held in both hands and worked backward and forward. As the grain is crushed, the flour is automatically sorted out and pushed forward into the basket in front, the heavier meal remaining on the flat stone. Sometimes, the Tuaregs use mortar and pestle. Spices or herbs are not used to flavor the food, with the exception of salt, and they often forget to use even this.

Once accepted by the people of the camp, I found my research into the social organization of these communities became easier. 1 found that festivals connected with important events were not exceptionally interesting. Birth occurred without any unusual celebration. Childbirth is natural and unassisted; there are neither local medicine men or midwives. Women in labor are attended by their older relations or intimate friends, whose assistance is limited to massaging the body with hands steeped in butter or fat. Newly-born children are wrapped in some ragged garment, but receive no special care. They are laid on a cushion of grass or leaves. Babies are carried on their mother's back, slung with one tiny leg on each side of the mother's waist in the fold of cloth which constitutes her skirt. The cloth is firmly rolled around the baby and the woman's body and tucked in over the breast. Only the child's head emerges from the pouch. As the child sleeps or cries or sucks its fingers the mother goes about her daily occupation pounding millet or plaiting mats.

According to Islamic custom the boys are circumcised at the age of a few months, but neither at birth or later in life is any form of bodily deformation practiced. marriages are not arranged. It often happens that a girl has two or more serious suitors, but she is free to make her own choice. It is common for a girl who is in love with a man to take a camel and ride all night to see him, and then return to her own people, or for a suitor to make expeditions of superhuman endurance to see his girl. Illicit love affairs inevitably occur, and If a child is born, the man is obliged to marry the woman. After the bridegroom has wooed his bride and paid the dowry, the marriage is celebrated with feasting and rejoicing. The dowry given to his wife on marriage by the husband varies from a few coins to several camels. This dowry remains the property of the wife for her lifetime. Even after divorce the husband cannot take the dowry back. In the married state the man or woman does not stop having intimacy with friends whom he or she likes, and it often happens that a man enters his tent to find his wife with a male friend. He will neither disapprove or make trouble.

The Tuaregs divorce less frequently than Western societies and this is carried out in accordance with the Islamic system, without publicity or fuss. carriage and divorce, according to Islamic law, is a human contract and can be broken under certain conditions. although divorce Is easier in Islamic society, the divorce rate is lower in Muslim countries than in Christian or non-Islamic countries.

One of the most exciting events of my stay at the camp was to be present at the "Ahal." It was a never-to-be-forgotten experience. The "Ahal" is not Just a social gathering. It is, in fact, a literary meeting, at which all the Tuaregs gather to recite and listen to poems. The Tuareg are natural poets and the women especially are given to the development of poetry and its preservations. The Ahal is always held at night, and at these desert meetings the poems are often accompanied by a musical instrument called the Amzad.

Often in the toil of modern life, I look back upon my memories of those nights in the Sahara when I sat with the Tuaregs and their women around the camp fire. I remember listening to the beautiful ballads accompanied by the plaintive daunting melodies of the Ahal.

Ibn Batutah, the great Arab philosopher and explorer, once went into a house of a judge and found him with a very beautiful young woman. As he stopped, doubting and hesitating, and wanting to leave, she began to laugh at his embarrassment He was shocked. There is a Tuareg proverb which says "Men and women towards each other are for the eyes and for the heart and not only for the bed." The consequences of such a frame of mind is that the men and women of the People of the Veil are often blessed or cursed with love so lasting, so sincere and so devoted, that it makes or mars a life.

The Land Of The Naked Giants

 HAD BEEN TRAVELING HUNDREDS OF MILES TO STUDY the life of the Dinkas, who could be called the naked giants of the Southern Sudan. Leaving the battered truck on which my guide Tom and I had gotten a lift, we began tracking our way through tall grass. Suddenly I was aware of a tall naked Dinka sitting perfectly still in the branches of a tree, decorated with the full war paint of a warrior. He exchanged a few words with Tom and then Boom - Boom -Boom - he began beating out a message on a small drug. As we reached the boundary of the village, were met by the village chief and two counselors who had been warned of our arrival by look-out men. I was informed that I was the first non-Dinka ever to visit this village. Not even a North Sudanese had ever set foot there. The Dinka's were far too wary of strangers after the scare of the mutiny in the Southern Province.

The chief was wearing a necklace of lion's claws, an ivory arm bangle, and a row of colored glass beads around his waist. He was otherwise naked. He carried a long, murderous-looking spear decorated with ostrich feathers. I wondered how many battles it had seen, and how many enemies, animal and human, it had slain. Tom had already informed the chief about my intended visit, and he seemed delighted to see me. I was introduced to all the villagers and taken to a guest hut which I was told would be mine for as long as I cared to stay.

The hut was comfortable compared to the pygmy huts. There was a leopard skin over a mattress of plaited grass and two earthenware pots used to contain food, as well as a goat's skin, which hung from the center pole, which contained drinking water.

The following day I was allowed to witness the ancient ceremony when a Dinka boy officially becomes a man. About twenty boys, naked like the rest of the tribe' marched in single file towards the village. They had been away for a month "proving" themselves, living in the marshes and supporting themselves by hunting and fishing. Drums beat a welcome for them as they returned to the village. They sat on the ground, with the entire village looking on while their heads were shaved. When this was over, each boy's father presented him with a spear, a harpoon for hunting hippos, and some beads and ornaments. This was followed by a special dance which the boys perform for the purpose of attracting the young village girls, and then they lined up for the gornum ceremony, in which tribal scars are marked on the forehead. The chief kissed the blade and then gashed the forehead of the boy that was held before him. Again and again the knife flashed in the African sun as blood streamed from their faces, making eight long, straight cuts. The boys only made a low, murmuring sound, nothing more. A witch doctor rubbed a special red ointment into the wounds made from cow dung and urine, fat, and some coloring.

It was a special thrill to observe this ceremony, for I had very much wanted to spend some time with these people and observe their customs first-hand. The early

Dinkas were mostly hunters and fishermen. They must have received their first domestic animal, the ox, somewhere around 4000 B.C from the Egyptians. I wondered why the Dinkas did not also import the idea of clothing from the Egyptians when they adopted some of their other customs. The Egyptians had used clothing as far back as 6000 B.C., although they were only animal skins at the time. This remained a curiosity to me, and I could only speculate that they thought the idea of clothing impractical in this tropical region.

Being a semi-nomadic tribe, the Dinkas have a permanent home which is used as a base and is situated on the high ground. It is permanently occupied by elderly people, who do not move with the cattle. They also have a dry-season camp which consists of straw huts, and a dung fire is kept burning in order to keep insects and mosquitoes away.

Their spear chief is the religious as well as the civil head of the tribe, and he performs the ceremony of rain-making. He carries a sacred spear which goes with his office and is handed down from generation to generation. He is elected by the people on the basis of heredity and ceremonially installed. He sits on an ambach bed and after the elders have bathed him, he is garlanded with ostrich egg shells and crowned with a ring made of the mane of an antelope. A bull is sacrificed and skinned to be used on his throne. The elders then cut a portion of the hide and proclaim loudly their loyalty to the spear chief. At the end of the ceremony, feasting begins and more bulls are sacrificed. This feasting may last for several days.

When the spear chief becomes old and unable to, he is ceremonially killed by the people. Generally, the spear chief is quite elderly when he receives his title, for it would be out of the question for a young man to take on such an important role and give orders to the elders of the tribe. The chief himself chooses the occasion of his death. He is suffocated to death in his hut either by his wives or sometimes the elders of the tribe, and then buried there. The Dinkas believe that if a spear chief dies from natural causes, his soul is lost forever. If he is ceremonially killed, his soul enters into the new spear chief, and during the period of transition from one chief to another, his soul guards the tribe. Should the chief die by accident or in war, the tribe sacrifices a sheep which is buried with him.

Another custom that I found interesting is that a Dinka is never permitted to marry a woman from his own clan, nor a woman related to him through his mother. The average bridal wealth consists of 20 to 100 heads of cattle, depending among the wealth of the family. A cow is distributed to the bride's mother, a calf to the maternal grandfather, and one goat for each of the mother's brothel In the case of divorce, the cattle of the bridal wealth is returned with their offspring. General reasons for divorce are inability to produce a child, adultery, or being a bad housewife. If a bride should die within two years of her marriage, the father of the bride supplies a younger sister as her substitute or returns the bridal wealth.

If a married Dinka should die without any children, or an unmarried man die, his kinsmen are duty bound to marry a woman in his name and have children who would still belong to the deceased man. Should a widow have no children or possess cattle, she will marry a girl in her husband's name and use the cattle as a dowry.

One of her husband's near relatives would then be asked to cohabit with the girl, and should a child be born, it would be named after the widow's husband. A widow can never remarry, and becomes the property of any brothers of her deceased husband or his son from another wife.

When the Dinkas bury their dead, they wrap the corpse in skins and bury it on the right side of the doorway of the person's hut. Then the father and brothers of the deceased man stay in the hut for three days and do not drink mile during that period. It is a general belief that when a Dinka dies, his soul, which is called "tiep," wanders around. Sometimes through dreams the tiep asks the relatives to give some sacrifices. The tiep is considered to be very powerful at the time of death, but weakens as time passes by.

Sorcery is not practiced much by the Dinkas, but the do practice this craft when they wish to do harm to another person. The Dinka takes an iron ring from his finger, which most wear, and places it on the grass, calling out the name of the enemy and breaks the ring in two. He buries one piece in the swamps and throws the other into a river or stream.

I was fortunate to see the rainmaking ceremony while at Tom's village. Dedgote is the god of rain. The spear chief comes out into the open, ceremoniously dressed, with a painted face and a whitewashed body, oil top of which some orange coloring has been added. He stood with his Sacred spear in his right arm and chanted some prayers. He then jumped twice into the air and bent forward three times, pointing his spear to the sky. After he had repeated this motion a few times, he shouted loudly. The prayer to Dengdote was then over, and a bull was sacrificed and everyone feasted while waiting for rain.

An ancestor's spirit may often haunt his relatives, so the victim of the haunting digs out the ancestor's body from the grave and removes one of his teeth, tying it onto his right arm. This saves him from further molestation. I could never discover if the same procedure is repeated should fresh spirits decide to haunt the same poor victim. I presumed that one tooth was sufficient to scare away all other spirits.

In the memory of a dead spear chief, the Dinkas build a shrine. Tom and I visited on about six miles from the village. We walked there early one morning to avoid the heat of the midday sun. The shrine was a sort of mould, made and plastered with earth, in the shape of a cone. Near the top of it were two bull's horns and a fence of mud in the shape of a low wall. The shrine was called Buro and surrounding it were many dozens of wooden pegs. The tribe visited this shrine fairly regularly to see to any repairs that may be needed, frequently taking their cattle with them to sacrifice a bull in the name of the spear chief. They usually stay there for a few days before returning to the village.

After we had visited the shrine, we decided to rest under a shady tree and I had a short nap before starting on our homeward journey. The whole area was adjacent to a game reserve. Tom was practicing his spear throwing when he suddenly shook me awake. I could see that he was very nervous and asked him what was the matter. In mortal terror, he said "Boll, Boll," and pointed towards a thick growth of thorny bushes. At first I could not see anything, but then I saw it - a large buffalo plastered with dried out mud. Fortunately he was not facing in our direction, but was only a hundred yards away or so. Tom and I dared not speak or even whisper, lest he detect our presence. In sign language, torn told me to slip quietly away and I readily obeyed, having no desire for my shrine to be erected on the spot. Slowly and cautiously, on hands and knees, we edged our way until we had reached a reasonably safe distance from the animal. When we finally stood up, we ran as fast as our legs would carry us towards the village. On reaching the village, I told Tom that it was not a "boll" but a "buffalo" that we had enconntered. He smiled and said "shakrum" (thank you) and when I asked him where he had learned this Arabic work he told me that it was in Khartoum.

As there were very few days left until my departure via steamer for Kosti, I asked Tom if I could visit a hippo colony, for one was not very far from the village. On arriving at the shores of the lake, I climbed a small hill from which I could see the Nile and the papyrus swamps. There was a small stream leading to the Nile flowing by the side of the hill on which we were standing. There were about 20 hippos in the lake, their dark brown glossy hides shining in the sun. Some were completely submerged in deep water, but quite a few were standing in the shallow end of the lake. There was one hideous bull hippo who was churning up the water in foam and waves. Another opened his mouth in our direction, showing four magnificent tusks sufficiently strong to crush a crocodile with practically no effort.

After a brief stay, we left the hippos and returned in peace to the village. I was lucky to see some of the Dinka cosmetics being prepared. Some of the coloring matter is obtained when one of the numerous grass fires pass over an ant hill, turning the surface of the blackish-grey clay into a red powder. This powder plays a major role in the Dinka's beauty preparations. The hair is curled with the aid of grass, and together with the whole body, is covered with a mixture of powdered red clay, cow urine, sheep's droppings and burnt cow dung. I could not go near a freshly-toiled Dinka because of the strong foul smell, but this paste serves its purpose in repulsing mosquitoes and insects, and removes the necessity to wear clothing.

The Dinka diet consists mostly of milk and kordalla, which are a variety of beans From these beans they make a flour of the seeds, which is then made into a paste and eaten with milk. A custom among some of the tribes is to remove a few of the front teeth during childhood by a painful process of tearing them out with a fish spear. I could not see any purpose in this procedure unless it was to facilitate the eating of the pastes.

One morning I observed another common practice. About half a dozen natives were tying the legs of a bull, and when he was securely tied, a young Dinka punctured a vein in the animal's neck with a sharp spear. Thick red blood spurted from the wound, which was immediately caught in special bowls. When these bowls had been sufficiently filled, the artery was compressed by means of the fat on the animal's neck and then pasted together with dung and wet clay. The bull was then left until the plaster had completely dried and the blood had stopped oozing from the wound. The bowls of blood were passed around for drinking, but I managed to politely refuse by placing a hand on my stomach to indicate that I was already full.

Among the native people of Central Africa, the belief of a form of a Supreme Being is-so strong that they have no fear of death, which I found to be very near the Islamic belief of life. So often foreign ideas are poured into the heads of the natives in an effort to teach the that their customs are wrong. A moment's thought will show the utter selfishness, and even cruelty, of taking away the pillar of strength afforded by even a pagan belief in a land of sudden and awful death, without substituting something equally strong so that no loss is felt at times of need. I am against imposing one's culture or values on others.

I talked with one of the Dinkas who was curious about life in big cities. I told him about the bright lights, the night life and the night clubs He wanted to know what went on in these clubs and I told him of the various cabaret shows and the act of strip-tease. He laughed heartily at my description and told me that he thought our civilized people were crazy to pay to see a naked woman. Surely all woman are alike, and did they not see their own wives! I am sure that a nudist organization would have been pleased to hear his remarks.

On many evenings I could hear the treacheries of wild hunting dogs. These animals have a hyena-like droop of the hindquarters, ending in an unusually bushy tail and very loose skin. They normally move in groups of 60 to 70 animals, but sometimes can be seen in packs as large as 200. They generally hunt after dawn and a few hours before sunset an sleep the remainder of the day. They are absolutely ruthless in their hunting. They move in total silence, encircling their game and then ripping open the leg or thigh. The craftiness of their organization betrays an intelligent aptitude for their work which is almost human in its mastery. The pack is always on the move and shows a general preference for bushy parts of the country.

On my departure from the village the chief presented me with a hippo harpoon, an ivory bangle which is worn by the natives to show manhood, and a few other small souvenirs In return for the hospitality shown to me, I presented the chief with a pocket watch and tried to explain its workings to him. He was very amused with this gift and asked me to explain the difference between three o'clock and four o'clock. I told him that at three o'clock only three hours had passed since the sun was overhead, and at four o'clock four hours had passed. He had great fun in learning this new technique and laughed a great deal when he discovered he could "reverse" time by setting the hands back on the watch. I laughed too, and thanked him for his hospitality.

The Land Of The Pygmies And The Watusies

RUWENZORI, OR "THE MOUNTAINS OF THE MOON," though situated on the equator, is still perpetually covered by glaciers and snow. This mountain, along with Kilimanjaro and Kenya, is among the highest mountains on the African continent. Even Ptolemy, who lived in the second century, knew that it was The Mountains of the Moon that fed the River Nile. Its origin, unlike Kilimanjaro and Kenya, was not due to volcanic upheavals but assumed to be due to global upheaval~ The flora varies from tropical vegetation to that found in polar regions, due to its non-volcanic origin, which has preserved the heritage of past ages.

I was eager to leave Stanleyville as quickly as possible, and one day a friend informed me that a car was going to Bukavu in Kivu and that I could accompany the driver as far as Goma on Lake Kivu.

The driver, a Belgian, picked me up at 8 a.m. I bundled my-luggage into the hack and clambered in beside him, offering my hand and introducing myself. I learned his name was Mr. Baltrop. During the first part of our journey we retraced part of the route I had taken to Beni. In fact, our first stop was Nia. We arrived in time for dinner and then went straight to our room to retire. I started to tell Baltrop about my experience with the Esamba during my previous visit, and just as I reached the climax of the story, discovered my companion was sound asleep, not having heard a word of my adventure.

The next morning we left early for the Ituri forest, the home of the Bambute pygmies whose features tally with the density of the forest. They stand only about four feet tall, are brown and very hairy, especially on the chat. The hair on their heads is mostly black and curly, though I have sometimes noticed a greenish-grey color on the back part of the scalp and a sometimes reddish-brown color on the forehead. Their eyes are prominently set and their faces are generally void of wrinkles, save perhaps a few on the forehead. Their noses are flat and wanting in bridge, while the nostrils are large and prominent, and the upper lip is long and very curved. The have long arms and short legs, and their big toes turn outward, leaving a big gap between the first and second toes.

Mutilation of the teeth is a wide-spread practice among the pygmies, many of whom file them down. As a rule, these little folk follow the mutilation practices of the neighboring Bantu tribes with the exception of circumcision. Also unlike their neighbors, they never scar or tatoo their bodies, nor do they adorn them with necklaces, bracelets, waist belts, or such like. When at home they wear nothing, but in public they wear a tiny piece of genet, monkey or antelope skin, or a piece of bark cloth.

The pygmies build little round huts to match their height, standing about three feet from the ground. These are constructed by planting thick ends of long flexible branches firmly into the ground and then bending the other ends over until they are almost rooted, the giving the appearance of a flat semi-circle.

These branches cross one another at the top, and the entire framework is covered with banana leaves or other kinds of large leaves and firmly secured. A small hole is left uncovered near the bottom to be used as an entrance.

Generally, each family member has their own hut, which is completely bare save for a few animal skins on which they sleep. Their main diet consist of game meal such as antelopes, monkeys and elephants, as well as various kinds of beans, bananas, edible wild fruits and nuts. Their main love is honey, and they take great pains to secure the honey combs by driving out the bees.

It is an anthropological belief that at one time the whole eastern half of Africa from the coast of the Red Sea to the southern tip of the continent was inhabited by the Bantu. I believe that at a later stage, when the Caucasians invaded the northern part of Africa, they exterminated the pygmies from that area and surrounding regions, and they were forced to take shelter in the great forests of the Congo. Here the pygmies adopted a way of life suitable to their environment and to a great extent were safer than the other Bantus of the open countryside who were captured and traded as slaves by succeeding invaders from Asia and Europe.

Baltrop and I reached Camp Putnam in time for breakfast. This camp was founded by Dr. Putnam, an anthropologist so he could study the pygmies in their natural habitat. He was also a health officer and established the camp as a hospital so he could treat the natives for different ailments. Opposite the camp was a zoo, or perhaps "depot" would be a more appropriate term. Animals who were caught in the forest were detained here before being shipped to various zoos around the world.

After breakfast, we pushed on again, passing crowded native villages of 10- to 20- leaf thatched huts. The natives walked in groups with bundles piled high upon their heads, their bare splayed feet kicking up the dust dried out by the morning winds. Often we passed baboons loping across the road and noticed hornbills flying among the trees, and blue bullikookoos rising lazily from the swampy areas along side the low timber bridges. We were passing trough an area that is home to the driver ants and the bolozi leopards. An explorer has to fight against these horrible creatures and has no alternative but to win in order to survive.

Driver ants give the impression of black lava pouring out of a volcano as they move. They travel in columns, mostly at night, moving very fast and eating everything that lies in their path. I have only seen them once, but that was quite sufficient. In Mambasa, I remember seeing the skeleton of a monkey whose bones were picked completely clean after having been overrun and eaten alive by a swarm of these ants, and have often perspired with horror at the thought of being treated in a likewise manner. A queen ant is roughly ten times larger than the others and her only purpose is to lay millions of eggs. She is born blind, while all the males have eyes in order to find her and mate. They are nomadic and forever on the move. The only way they die is when the humidity drops below 40 percent.

We stopped for a short while at Mambasa and then carried on the Beni. This small town is situated under the Ruwenzori and is the starting point for the ascent to the mountain. We stayed there for a few days and then began our climb up the small Karibumba escarpment. On reaching the top, we had a majestic view of the equatorial forest. We passed trough the Luhule valley, which is covered with elephant grass and occasionally caught glimpses of herds of pachyderms who had left the forest to seek out young vegetation.

At the head of the valley we stopped for a couple of hours at Butebo and then proceeded to Lubero, crossing the equator. From here we saw a magnificent panorama of the high plateau of Wanuande with scattered villages and banana plantations. The evening was clear, and as the sun set, it gave the mountains and forest a bluish-green tint. The glaciers were like a river full of oranges. It was beautiful beyond description.

Before arriving at Lubero, we took the eastern road and traveled on the Congo Nile ridge of Mt. Lubue, crossing the highest point of our trip at 7400 feet. The -mountains were covered with pines and bamboo whose branches were laden with hanging moss. This region is homeland to the gorilla The bamboo shoots are a delicacy for these animals, and they also have a great liking for bananas, frequently raiding neighboring plantations.

We entered the Albert National Park in the early hours of the evening. This park was established in 1925 and it was created by King Albert of Belgium, who wanted the natural wealth of the country preserved for the benefit of scientific research, tourism and the protection of wild life. The park is home to the gorilla, okapi, rhinoceros, elephant, kudu, leopard, lion, giraffe, eland, chimpanzee, a variety of monkeys and antelopes, hippopotamus, zebra, wild ass, buffalo, ostrich, crocodile, and a large number of wild birds, including the secretary bird, the loud hornbill, and the flamingo. It is surrounded by the Graben Rift on Lake Kivu, which is about 180 miles long and 30 miles wide. Roughly speaking, this park covers the plains south of Lake Edward, -including the lake, the whole chain of Virunga volcanoes, and the Semliki and Ruwenzori mountains.

We decided to spend the night at the Ruindi Camp, which is on the Ruindi Plain, a wooded savannah surrounded by wildlife. We started to descend down the zig-zag road, and had hardly driven a mile when the car's headlights picked out some obstacle in the middle of the road. As we approached it, we discovered the obstacle to he a mighty hippo, at least one and a half tons in weight. I asked Baltrop to stop the car so I could take one or two photographs of him, and was just resting my camera on the hood of the car to steady it when he started moving towards us. Baltrop shouted and put the car into reverse before I even had time to get in. He seemed much more terrified than I, even though he was seated safely inside the car while I clung to the hood. The hippo, however, didn't take us very seriously and retreated into the grassy swamps beside the road. We waited for about ten minutes until Baltrop was quite certain we would not be paid another visit before we proceeded. We experienced no further delays before reaching the Ruindi Camp, but we did catch a few glimpses of buffalo and an elephant a few yards from the roadside.

On reaching the camp we discovered it to he completely full, and had no alternative but to drive straight on through the night until we reached God A few miles outside of camp, a leopard dashed in front of our car and was momentarily dazzled by our headlights. He

An Indian From Rio Negro In Brazil

An Aymara Girl From Lake Titicaca

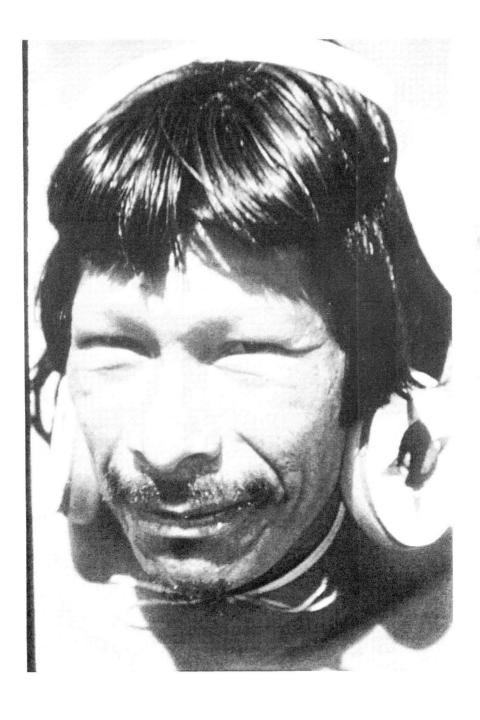

A Cofano Indian From Amazon Basin

Tuaregs From Sahara

A Rickshaw Driver In China

A Street Tailor In China

A Village In The Sahara Desert

A Nubian Woman Of Upper Nile

started running ahead of us in the center of the road, remaining in the path of our lights, but on rounding a bend he disappeared into the grassy plain. He was our last companion in the National Park, and I thoroughly enjoyed his brief visit with us.

Our next stop was at Rutshwin, a small town situated on the river of the same name, in the mouth of the Virunga chain of volcanoes. We stopped only briefly for refreshment and then continued to Goma. A few miles further on I could see the red glow of the skyline of Nyiragongo, one of the two active volcanoes in this chain, and could clearly see smoke rising. We reached Goma in the early hours of the morning and after a very quick shower climbed straight into bed, exhausted after our long drive.

Goma was a small town, but unforgettably beautiful, set in the most picturesque of surroundings. It is situated on Lake Kivu at an altitude of 4800 feet and is the district capital of Kivu-Nord. This lake is the highest in Central Africa and is spread over an area of 1000 square miles. It is full of otters but there is not much fishing to be had, nor are there many crocodiles or hippos. The northern end of the lake is wooded, while the southern has plains mostly covered with banana plantations. In 1938, the volcano Nyamulagira erupted and lava cut across the Goma.Sake road, reaching the lake and destroying everything in its path, including Mayutsa, a small government post.

While in Gomo, I met a charming lady who had been a director of tourism in East Africa for many years, organizing safaris. Her name was Madame Bania. She arranged for transportation for me to the mandated territory of Randa-Urandi, where the majority of inhabitants belong to the Watusi and Warundi tribes. Baltrop was to remain in Gomo, and without her assistance i would have had no means of transport.

I found that except for the Ruzizi Plain, the countryside of the Ruanda-Urandi territory was mostly mountainous, and the main occupation of the people there was cattle breeding. The Watusi and Warundi tribes are of Hematic origin, and because they treat their cattle as sacred animals, they have something in common with the ancient Egyptians, who worshipped Aphis, the bull. A Ruandan will never kill his cattle for meat, which was quite a different practice from the Masai, who keep his cattle alive while simultaneously drinking its blood by puncturing the veins in the neck.

The Watusi tribe are the giants of Central Africa, averaging about six and half feet. They are mostly very dark-skinned and greatly resemble Ethiopians, with the exception of their size. The Watusi dancers are very famous in Africa. They carry spears and wear red and white cotton skirts with headdresses made of beading and monkey hair. Around their ankles they wear- anklets that have bells attached.

On my return from Usumbura, the capital of Ruanda-Urandi, I decided to visit the countryside surrounding the active volcanoes. On the northeast of Kivu they are called the Virunga and separate the Nile and Congo basins by cutting across the whole width of the Central Graben Rift. There are eight, ranging in height from 10,000 feet to nearly 15,000 feet. The two active ones are called Nyiragongo and Nyamlegira. The legend of the Nyiragongo volcano is that it was named after a native woman by some of the people who died in that area, and her spirit is meant to haunt the spot. It is believed that all the souls of the damned are sent to the volcano to atone for their skins in the perpetual fires, while the souls of the pure are sent to the summit of Karisimbi with the white snow.

I wished to climb Nyamulagira, so I returned to Goma to secure permission and obtain a porter and guide from a nearby village. From Kakomero, which is situated at an altitude of 5900 feet, I continued to Mushumangabo at 6840 feet. The climb took a little over an hour. I found a hut for shelter in which to spend the night, and the next morning saw an old tusker drinking from a nearby pond. It was a marvelous sight. Unfortunately, he noticed me and retired into the bush quickly. The track crossed moss- and lichen-covered lava, above which was the most beautiful forest of the region. The podocarpus tree grows here, which is one of the rare resinous trees of Africa, with dark green shining lanceolate leaves and which can attain a height of 60 to 70 feet. I also saw some beautiful mauve orchids.

After a five-hour climb, I reached the crater and spent my second night in its shelter. Entering a crater is like entering a cave with vertical walls. Insider there were huge pits which pour out sulphurous gasses, smoke and steam. I found the volcanoes not only interesting because of their beauty, but also they provide us with great knowledge on geology, seismology and volcanology. After collecting a few specimens, I returned to the base and then back to Goma.

I found bird life abundant in the Kivu region, and saw large and splendid turacos, sun birds and parrots. During the afternoon I could see banks of moving cumulus clouds, tinged with rose and grey and gold, piled high in the western sky. The sun, with shafts of brilliant light driving through the clouds, smote the glassy lake and cast down cloud shadows like phantom rudderless boats of purple, violent and deep lapis lazuli, to drift slowly and capriciously across the quite surface of the water. The bright mountains rising above and beyond the shore took on a misty blue, and in the defiles revealed the sane contrasts and varieties of color abounding in the lake. It reminded me of a Persian saying engraved on a famous building in India: "If there is heaven on earth, the here it is, here it is, and here it is."

During the next few days I wandered over the lava fields in search of some interesting lava species along the Goma-Sake road. The Kivu area was like a paradise for me. Everything that I had wanted to study was at hand; the people, the wildlife, the flora and fauna, all accumulated in one small area, and beautiful beyond words. Shouldn't I say that paradise is beyond the Mountains of the Moon?

The Land Of The Chinese Peasant

N A RECENT VISIT TO CHINA I TOOK EVERY OPPORTU-
nity to get out into the countryside. Everywhere
I found it fascinating, varying greatly in different
parts of this vast country. More than seven hundred
million people live in the country in China, producing
food for the towns and cities as well as themselves. In
days gone by it was a precarious living, where many of
the peasants had little land and some none at all, and
nearly everyone hopelessly in debt to landlords and
money lenders. One result was that every square inch of
land that could possibly bear a crop was diligently
cultivated, including tiny corners, bits of railway
embankment, the bottom of dry ditches, and even
abandoned quarries.

Today things are different. One can still see little bits
of cultivation, but this is more a hangover from the past
and from recent years when there was a drought for
three consecutive years. The entire countryside of China
is now organized into- communes, 75,000 of them, and
farming is done on a large scale. Outside Beijing I came
across a commune of 25,000 people; near Guangzhou
there was one of nearly 50,000. Many are much smaller,
but in each one the land is cultivated by all the people,
according to a plan made by experts in the commune,
so that the bet use is made of the land and the most
successful crops are grown.

I found that although much of the work on the land is still done by human labor because a country of this size cannot be mechanized overnight, it is being done scientifically, with vastly increased irrigation, chemical fertilizers, better quality seeds and so on. On each commune I visited, there were modern laboratories and some really modern equipment, with men and women who were trained in various branches of agriculture. Enormous increases in production are being obtained, much of it due to a well-regulated water supply. A large commune near Guangzhou has already built four huge reservoirs and many smaller ones. The director told me that they would never fear a drought in the future - their irrigation water was secure. Near Shanghai another commune had increased its vegetable production four times in as many years, its wheat production three times, and nearly all due to having water available when it was most needed. Looking down from a plane between Beijing and Guangzhou, I could see large reservoirs all over the country for hours on end, often four or more in view at the same time.

In days gone by, a severe drought in China invariably meant that thousands and often millions of people died from starvation. Food ran out and none was available from anywhere else. During this recent very severe drought, it is doubtful if a single person in all China died from want of food. The stricken areas were supplied from those not affected, and although there were shortages, everyone had enough to live on. The present government is probably the first in Chinese history that is really interested in seeing that the people do not want for food in difficult times, and they plan accordingly.

Railways have been increased on an unbelievable scale in China in the last 30 years, so that now every province is connected with the rest of the country by rail. Chinese villages look much the same as always, but there are certain differences.

Many new houses are being built in the traditional style, with small gardens where the peasants may grow anything for their own consumption or to sell on the open market. There are schools everywhere, for the education of the children is the responsibility of the commune itself. There are also tractor stations and machinery repair shops. In some of them I saw small farm machines being made, often on a large scale. This is a great help and is likely to continue for many years, until the factories catch up with the unlimited demand for machinery and transport of very kind. Instead of peasants working individually on tiny plots of land, they now work in teams and brigades in big fields.

All this means far more efficiency on the land, and greater prosperity for the people. They are paid according to the work they put in, partly in kind, in the way of rice and other crops, partly in money, usually at the end of a year. I saw many houses where there were new radio sets, decent furniture, pictures on the wall, and bicycles for riding to work and to the nearest town. Such things were rare indeed until recently. The -people work hard and they do not own land of their own, except for their small plots around the house, but they see conditions getting better every year, and as far as I could tell, they seemed to be satisfied.

Much of the countryside is really beautiful, especially in the south among the rice fields of the Pearl River delta. Peasants still take their buffaloes to the fields to work, and they still wear the wide-brimmed straw hats that are so typical of China. I saw much variety in scenery as I went about the country on trains. In the mountains on the way to Choingoing, there were strange rock formations and cliffs with houses excavated in them, deep gorges and vast, swift rivers. Around Shanghai the land is flat again, wheat alternating with rice. In Manchuria, now known as Northeast China, the winds of -early winter were blowing the dust across the fields in spirals and tearing at the tall stalks of sorghum waiting to be gathered in. Amidst the hills around Hangchow girls were picking tea bushes, for this district is famous for the best green tea.

But, the countryside in China is not all farming and hard work. Much of it is for -recreation and holidays. Hangchow, Soochow and Wusih are holiday resorts of great beauty, with green hills, lakes, islands, streams and woodlands. In amongst the hills are ancient temples and pagodas, often very old and all now carefully preserved. Near Beijing are the Western Hills and the Fragrant Hills, with lovely temples and monasteries, were many people go on their days off. And of course there are the Ming Tombs and the Great Wall, which stretches for 2000 miles all across the mountains of northern China.

Everywhere, all over this vast land, the Chinese people are friendly and polite, and delightfully curious to see a foreigner in their midst. I believe I caused much pleasure to some of these people when I asked to see their homes; I know I made the day for many a school child when I went into their classrooms. This was often an uncanny experience. The children are so well disciplined that not a head would be turned in my direction when I went into a school. Then, at a word from the teacher, suddenly all children looked at me, broke into broad smiles and clapped loudly. I soon learned that I must clap back in acknowledgment of their greeting.

My lasting impression of China will be of the smiling children everywhere, healthy looking, not well-dressed, but never in rags, full of fun but never rowdy. And the people in general, so eager to talk to me, a foreigner. One old man came up to me in a park in Shanghai and said: "Welcome to my country." I complimented him on his excellent English and he said: "Oh, yes, I took my degree at Glasgow University and lived for many years in England."

The Land Of The
Burmese Hill Tribes

HE AIR FRANCE FLIGHT N.174 LANDED AT 11:50 A.M. in Bangkok. This journey is taking me to Burma. After checking into the Royal Orchid Sheraton I went to Union of Burma Airline for a seat for Rangoon. "None available today, try tomorrow," I was told. Got lucky and got a seat on UB.221 for Rangoon. After going thorough Immigration and Customs, I took a taxi to the Strand Hotel but it was full. So, I put my name on a waiting list and checked in at Kandawgyi Hotel located on a small lake outside the center of the town. In the meantime, I went to the Mausoleum of Emperor Bahadur Shah II, the last Mughal Emperor of India, who died in exile in Rangoon.

Two days after my arrival in Rangoon I got a call from Strand Hotel that my room was available. I was so glad. The receptionist very kindly gave me Room No.114 overlooking Rangoon River. It was a large room with a large bathroom and a huge balcony.

Next thing I have to do is to arrange my passage to Mandalay and Mayamo north of Rangoon. While waiting for the passage I visited the very interesting Bogyoke Market, Shew Dagon Ragoda and the local sights. A hundred years ago Burma was in the British Empire. I decided to take a train for Prome. We travel through hour after hour of countryside. I could see Water buffalo lumber about, young rice grows piercingly and on almost every rise there is the curve of a stupa.

Prome was once the capital of Burma. Almost every Burmese town has once been the capital, because when a new king took over he was usually so fearful of threats to his person that he had his nearest relatives murdered and then moved the capital. But all the ex-capitals have one thing in common, they are all stone's through from River Irrawaddy, because it was the backbone of the country for hundreds of years.

The British also carried on this tradition when they arrived. Not only did they move the capital from Mandalay to Rangoon, they built up a river flotilla of hundreds of vessels to ply up and down the river.

From Prome I caught a boat for Mandalay. The river at Prome is sluggish and wide. The sheer joy of moving up a big riyer outweighs everything else - you can always see something new on the banks - pagodas perched on unlikely outcrops river birds, farmers cultivating the new foreshore in the six months they have before the river rises again, and village women washing.

The Buddist monks with the shaven heads look like Telly Savalas and Yul Brynner. Almost everywhere the boat stops and puts out a plank and people run up and down it and then go off again. It is a long-distance boat and a local bus service as well. It may also be useful way to cross river if you can't catch a ferry; in hundreds of miles between Prome and Mandalay there is not a single road bridge. Some people got off at Pakoka, some got on. There is little sailing in the night and if there is then the captain would switch on a huge searchlight, the beam of which it attracted huge crowds of insects. When the searchlight was not on I used to stay out on deck smoking my pipe, but with the searchlight on, I could not stay out to enjoy my pipe as well at night while sailing in Arawady river. I had the a similar experience while sailing on the mighty river Amazon from Belem to Manaus.

The next major stop was for Pagan. It is an amazing sight in Burma. Across 40 sq. km of the country stretching back from Irawaddy, there are hundreds of Pagados and temples. Everywhere you look they are ruins of all shape and sizes. The main town of the Pagan area is about 5 or 6 km up the river and it is called Nyaung-Oo from Pagan. But, due to shortage of time I did not go down to visit Pagan and continued to Mandalay.

Once past the waterfront, Mandalay emerges as a city of green and leafy charm, a huge garden suburb awash with bicycles. After checking in to the Mandalay Hotel and having a good shower, I was ready to explore the city.

King Mindon founded the city in 1857. Mindon was succeeded by King Thibaw who was deposed by British when they occupied Burma. Mandalay was taken by British in 1885 and the capital moved to Rangoon, 716 km to the south. Mandalay has most of the structure made of wood which is plenty abundant in Burma.

The first place I wanted to visit was the main market where you see people in all shapes and costumes coming to market and you observe their trend of shopping. I came to the Zegyo Market. This market is a fascinating collection of stalls selling every sort of Burmese ware. It is typical Asian manner there are sections for everything, from jewelry, materials, books, or hardware etc. After wondering in the market I continued down 26ᵗʰ Road.

Beyond the market you eventually come to the river front, a scene of constant activity and interest. The 26th Road ends here.

Then, I proceeded to C Road north of the Mingun jetty and I saw the water buffaloes working in the fields. Mandalay streets are also full of horse-carts, similar to Tongas in India and Pakistan and another typical transport is Trishaws with passengers sitting back to back.

After a snack on the road I headed for Mandalay Hill. I approached from the south where two covered stairways wind their way up the hill and I reached the top. I could see for miles. Near the top was a huge standing Buddha image looking out towards the old royal palace. The legend says that Buddha himself visited the hill. He prophesied twenty four thousand years ago that a great city will be built here.

Close to the southern entrance to the hill stands the Kyauktawgy Pagoda and here is Buddha carved from a single block of marble. Around the shrine are the figures of the Buddha's eighty disciples. Mandalay's biggest festival is held here in the middle of October each year.

The Royal Palace was burnt out since, and today is the military encampment surrounded by walls which are eight meters high and three meters thick at the bottom. The palace was far more than just royal quarters - it was really a walled city within the city. Where the original palace was, now stood a raised platform and on it now is a museum. To the east of this platform is the ruins of a clock tower.

After visiting many more Pagodas I decided that my time on my visa was running out and I could not go northeast to Shan State from here, I took a return flight through Union of Burma Airline back to Rangoon and went to my favorite Strand Hotel and found it fully booked, so I had to go to Inya Lake Hotel about six km from the centre. This is an unimpressive hotel, but I got a room and the next day I took Thai International flight to Bangkok and change to the domestic flight to Chaing Rai heading towards the Thai-Burma boarder which is officially closed to foreigners, including me, but then I believe that "where there is a will, there is a way" and I crossed the boarder heading into Shan State of Burma.

The history of the tribes that I was interested is not a written script but it is preserved in poetry which for centuries have been transmitted orally, generation by generation along an unbroken chain of masters and pupil and have the status akin to that of a teacher or priest. Most of these tribes originated in Tibet and then stage by stage immigrated south to Burma and Yunnan in China, possibly in early centuries of A.D. Most of their tongue belongs to Tibeto-Burmese group.

Their main occupation is to grow rice in paddy fields, using water buffaloes to pull plows and also hunting in the forests, where they found boar, deer and bear. Their trade was tobacco, and dried chili peppers which were traded for iron and salt.

They are required to have prudent behaviors which also means observing the ritual requirements evolved by the generations of ancestors. From their home in the Ancestral Village, where all dead hope to return, the ancestors maintain a lively interest in the living, even though they play no active role. The living therefore must turn to the dead for guidance and pay due reverence by showing respect to tradition. In their ceremonies they offer food and drinks ceremoniously.

I spent some time in a village whom I will call Bawho in fact has a different name. The decision to use fictional name was made to protect the vulnerable villages from unwanted visitors.

I arrived at Santikhiri a village near the Burma border once occupied by KMT and United Shan Army. Eventually the Thai military made them to vacate this area. Most of the people in this area still speak Yunnanese because of the nearness of the Provence of Yunnan in China. Some local hill tribes here are Akha. The main cash crop of this area is tea, corn and fruit trees. Another local specialty is Chinese herbs, called Yaa Dong.

Santikhiri in unlike any other town, with southern Chinese style house. There are other hill tribes in the vicinity like Lisu, Mien, and Yao. In the village I stayed in an old Chinese hotel called Chin Sae. It is all wooden Chinese affair. The food served here is Yunnanese rice noodle and spicy chicken curry. After a few days I rented a old jeep with a driver to take me to Mae Sai, the most northern point in Thailand. The border is divided by River Saim, the other side of the river is Burma from here a track leads to Tachilek in Burma. Generally foreigners are not allowed to cross the bridge on the river Sai to go into Burma but there is always some exceptions if one wants to take a challenge that if caught by Burmese official there might not be a return trip into Mai Sai. During my stay in Mai Sai I met a guide who agreed to smuggle me into Burma to visit Shan State.

All this area is mountains and track is up and down and I have to avoid the main track for personal security. There is also a large band of bandits operating in the area who would have loved to relieve me of my valuable possessions if I am carrying anything with me. I did not have a camera, watch or expensive belts or new clothes. My backpack consisted of everything well worn and not worth having except I had to carry currency for payments. The narrow trail would follow a mountain ridge for few miles then dip down to the stream-bed in a fold between two mountains and ascend again. It is very exhausting to labor up and over ridges bent under the weight of my backpack.

When the nightfall came myself and my guide had to find shelter beside the track under the huge trees to sleep. My object was to reach a village about 50 or 60 miles inside the Burma boarder. When in the daylight, I passed any small village in the clearing of the forest we stopped for a welcome meal of rice and vegetables, washed down with many cups of rice liquor, similar to Japanese Saki.

My destination was a village in Shan State. The Shan had been in revolt against the central government of Burma and had succeeded in establishing a tentative autonomy in eastern Burma. We were near the main track that goes from Kengtung to Thai border.

I passed several springs along the track, each one carefully tapped with open bamboo pipes supported by forked sticks. Next to the mouth of each pipe there is usually a bamboo cup up-ended on a stick, so that all who passed could have a drink which one needs it on these mountain travel on foot. This amenity is provided by the nearest village for the thirsty travelers.

At last exhausted I with my guide arrived late evening at the village of Baw Ho hidden in the jungle clearing on near top of a mountain ridge. I waited outside the Village gate and my guide went inside the village to see the headman of the Village to explain my purpose of my visit and if I am welcome to stay a little while to know about the daily life of the village people. The village headman told him I can stay with them but I must promise not to mention the name of the village or its location for the purpose of the safety of the Village families. He explained that if the guerrillas found out that a foreigner has stayed in the village they will think the villages have received money and they will raid the village and loot it. Also I should not wander out too far from the village boundary or be seen by the guerrillas or we all will be in bad trouble and the last thing I do not have to pay for is my stay and food.

After a long wait, it is already dark now my guide comes back and we entered the village. The Headman met me and showed me the hut we will stay and I told him through my guide - interpreter that I will pay for my and my guides food and lodging with money, and I thanked him for his hospitality and permission to stay with them an we will not disturb the daily life of the village. They can continue doing what they normally do everyday. He asked me would I like to eat anything and I said I would like to go straight to lie down as I am very tired and I will eat tomorrow.

At the crack of dawn I was awake. I opened the bamboo door to look around a morning mountain mist obscured the village. Although it was not rainy season, but it did rain in the night and even the nearest huts were shrouded in low-lying clouds.

I would like to describe briefly the construction of a typical village house. The wooden house is built on poles dug well into the ground and strong enough to bear the weight of the house and inhabitants. On the poles rest a large wooden platform and the roof is all thatched. Then the house is divided into men and women's quarters and they have separate entrances, climbing on the platform by means of a short wooden ladder. Average house contains six or more people. The walls and the space under the roof is used for storage purpose. The platform hold space for bedding and baskets, food is dried above the fire and utensils are kept on wooden shelves.

Outside the men's entrance an open verandah provide a space to sit and where cloth and food also can be dried. The family and visitor can sit and talk. Under the platform of the house which could be about six feet space from the ground is used for women's rice-pounding mortar and also family animal pets can stay in rainy season. The cooking hearths on either side of the partition.

I heard a young girl of 13 or 14 years was pounding rice early morning for the day's food. I walked to see the procedure. The heavy beam of the mortar rode up in the slots of two supporting posts and hit the top with a crash. After pounding the unhusked rice in the mortar for half hour, the young girl propped up the pestle with stick and removed the grain in the mortar, scooping it out on the winnowing tray of loosely woven bamboo strips. She carried this tray out and began tossing the grain into the air with a light motion. She seems to enjoy this part of her performance. The rice being heavier fell back into the tray, the husk fell past the end of the tray on to a mat at her feet. This would be used to feed the pigs and chickens.

In Shan State opium poppy is grown because it has strong cash incentive of all hill community. The poppies bloom between November and February, depending on the variety, then the petals fall away, leaving an egg-shaped pod containing the milky opium sap. The women score the pods with a sharp knife. A day later the men scrape off the resin, dark with oxidation, that oozes from the pod, before packing it into banana leaf parcels ready for buyers from Thailand Burma and China to arrive for purchases.

Opium primarily is used by these hill tribes as an effective medicine for dysentery, malaria, rheumatism, diarrhea and excessive hunger pangs, but also smoke for pleasure. Their main diet is rice, banana, ginger, and tomato. For meat they occasionally eat chicken, buffalo, pigs, and rat. The chopsticks are commonly used for eating. They make rice liquor and bitter forest tea.

The role of the man is working in the fields or making things for the household needs, hunting and also meat cooking. Women run the household, when not working in the field. Getting up first each morning to make sure, it is well stocked with essentials , water, rice, firewood, fodder for the livestock. They also grow cotton to make cloth, do the embroideries and mending garments. Their day is spent after household chores in stitching, spinning, bead-stringing and sitting a talking with other village women, or if there is dance in the evening then all men and women of the village take part in it.

The courtship and romances starts at the dance sessions. The moral conventions permit young couples to wander off into the forest, provided they are not so closely related as to preclude an eventual marriage. If a relationship prospers and a marriage is arranged, the young couple will go into the forest for a few days to have sex before the wedding as a sort of pre-nuptial honeymoon. Some tribes have freedom to choose the partner they want, other tribes may have arranged marriages.

Husband and wife according to the custom do not have sex on day of inactivity after rice planting. No hunting, no field work, no sex. A complete rest on this so called inactivity day which is observed after the rice has been planted in the field. This custom does not apply for non-married young people, they can wander off together in the forest to have sex, they start having sex at around fifteen.

Silversmithing, is a great traditional crafts among most of the hill tribes of Shan States and also the hill tribe of Thai-Burma border. Most of this art is acquired from China during the migration from Tibet. They produce pieces of silver by hammering, buckles incised with abstract representation of birds, fish, butterflies, dragons, tigers, flowers, sun and moon motifs. They are produced in the elegant simplicity of form. They also produce superb bracelets.

With the advents of local bandits, jewelry is not worn when walking outside their villages. The women keep their silver jewelry hidden in the huts or underground and use aluminum ornaments for daily wear. On festive occasions the real silver ornaments are on view.

A Shaman treats his villagers through a seance, which may last all night in the privacy of his hut. For his services he is provided with eggs, tobacco, bananas, rice liquor, rice and some silver by the patient.

While I was there I heard that the Burmese Military was on the move towards North and it was the time for me to get out of Shan State.

The Burma's military regime has stepped up its attack on indigenous minorities. Millions of Karen, Shan, Karenni Arakan, and Mon people who live in mountain highlands that from Burma's boarder with Thailand, Laos, and China.

In these remote regions there are no cities or highways, only thousands of small villages, connected by narrow foot paths that wind through dense tropical forests. One woman told me when Burmese soldiers arrives in their village they loot all the food or other valuables they can find and then they force the women to haul supplies up the steep slopes and when the night comes they rape them.

Burma sells foreign logging companies the rights to log in the areas occupied by hill tribes and the money they get from lodging companies they buy arms and use them against the hill tribes who live peacefully in humble villages in the beautiful forested highlands and when the forests are gone, the tribes will fade away forever.

The Land Of The Ahagger

HE FIRST TIME I VISITED SAHARA DESERT WAS IN 1956 and then I visited again as the Leader of Sahara Recon. Expedition in 1957 with nine people from England and a book was published in London, "Desert Welcome" and also I produced a Television Documentary film for European TV Network.

This journey to Ahaggar was my third trip into Sahara, the world's largest desert. Sahara has played an enormous role in history. Its vastness is almost inconceivable - 3500 miles from Atlantic coast to the coast of the Red Sea. My destination was the Mediterranean coast to Tamanrasset. I traveled with another European employed by an Oil Company from Europe. We traveled in the English Land Rover stopping in oasis en route.

Despite its bleakness, the Sahara is a land of great beauty, as any travelers to the desert will readily admit, found startling contrasts of the desert's varied landscapes: the "chaos of peaks and needles" if the Ahaggar massif which the sun transforms from funeral black into mountains that seem to burn with "an interior fire." The 700 mile long Tassili ridge whose crags appeared to men camped beneath to be medical fortress: the oasis with their date palms of deep green nestled among powder gold dunes.

Even today it is true that the inhabitants need no map to travel in this great desert. We took the route from Tripoli to Ghadames to In Salah in the broad Tuat oasis and from there south to Timbuktu in Mali. The most dangerous part of the route is between Tuat and Ahagger and Timbuktu. The travel in Sahara is a murderous business. The distances are vast, the terrain brutal, and weather pitiless. Heat is the major enemy in the land where in winter days it is 100°F and in the summer the temperature of 150°F and above is not uncommon. In the night the temperature drops to 60°F. The winter temperature in the higher altitudes of the Ahagger often drop below freezing. Also some years it snows there too.

To the discomfort I suffered with the extreme temperature is often added with the ordeal of the sandstorm. Suddenly, the wind rasps, driving the small particles of sand before it like birdshot. The noise is horrible. The worst thing about a sandstorm is that the scorching Scirocco simply intensifies the torturing thirst. My throat was on fire and my tongue clove the roof of my mouth. The only thing I thought of was water, lakes, streams coming down from the mountains. In summer, a man needs to drink two gallons of water daily so we have to carefully ration.

One time during this journey it rained and rained within five minutes it was raining cats and dogs and a dry stream bed was flooded and we could not cross it with the Land Rover because of the force of the water. The water color was red and full of sand splashed from rock to rock. The Wadi carries its muddy water with a sound of violent wind.

One can not carry enough water to last the journey the Saharan roads zigzag across the desert going from one well to another. There we have to refill our water containers till we reach the next oasis. These wells are often no more than holes in the ground sometimes it is difficult to detect them as often they are camouflaged by rocks by the desert men themselves and they could be easily missed. My friend was not enjoying the trip at all but I enjoyed all the way just watching the natures wonderland in spite of the extremes of temperature and the so called roads, which were mostly rocky surface marked by blocks of stones and that is it.

Here and there when the sand uncovers human skeleton could be seen, who must have parished because of thirst, heat, or sandstorm. You first look at it and keep going, no use of burying it again if the nature wants to expose it to tell the passerby what can happen in this great desert.

One thing one must not do to look at the water too critically when you draw it from the well with a rope and a bucket. Sometime the water has sulfuric taste, but its is still the precious water. The main diet of the desert people I came across who were traveling in a camel caravan was dried dates, a handful of ground millet mixed with water a little fat for flavoring, which might be patted into small cakes and salt. Most of the fruits and grain is cultivated in the oasis. When a plague of locusts takes place, people gather these locusts and eat them boiled or fried with little salt and pepper in oil, as one does like shrimp. For a hungry and starving men, the appearance of food, no matter how revoltingly prepared, vanquished any squeamishness.

When I was invited by Desert hosts, with them we ate with anything less than total gluttony, but that is just another of the Saharan ironies. You might drown in the world's most arid region freezing in the earth's furnace and overeat in a land which could hardly produce a bean or leaf.

I find to travel in the Sahara it is required mental toughness and determination of an extraordinary order progress day after grueling day over this naked and hostile land, only when one sees an oasis full of greening and water channels irrigating the fields finding a paradise found.

The thing that surprised me was the nomad of Sahara who is illiterate questioned by me drew an intelligible map with his fingers in the sand: he has a highly developed sense of topography and direction for these as the matters of life or death to him.

Speaking in general terms, the Sahara is a region relatively barren in character: that lacks in any form of life. In this respect, it is the strict sense of the word a true desert, even from the viewpoint of human habitation.

There are some remnants of humanity clinging tenaciously to certain small corners of the Sahara. The truly Saharan nomads are all exclusively camel herders. They are known as Tuaregs. Tuaregs, unlike other tribes settled in oasis who do farming, have a marked individuality of their own. Representing only a small fraction of the human race, they have nevertheless a world-wide notoriety which may be partly owing to chance and the mysterious glamour of their desert background. In spite of the fact that they are Berbers and belong tot he Caucasian race. Their dress is always black or dark blue, and what is even more striking like them they wear the Litham or famous Saharan veil which mask the entire face except for the eyes and is rarely removed. On one occasion I persuaded them to remove the veil for me to photograph them. I have written about them in more detail in an earlier chapter under the title of "The Land Of The Veiled Men."

We were approaching the Ahaggar, whose summit is a kind of eroded platform with lava fields predominating. The platform is called the Atakor of Ahaggar by the Tuaregs or the Kudia by the Arabs. It is 155 miles in greatest diameter and maintains an altitude of some 6,600 ft in all parts, with extinct volcanoes jutting above the general level of almost 9,900 ft and it is called Mt. Ilaman.

We passed through Amguid Gorge. Wedged between a long chain of dunes to the west and twisted rocks of all shapes. There is a stream at the bottom of the gorge. This was the first running water which I have met in this Saharan journey. We stopped here for a couple of days before starting toward our goal Tamanrasset. From here the dark foothills of the Ahaggar were invisible to the south.

The Ahaggar is the Tuareg heartland, it is a land that appears desolate yet Ahaggar is far from uninhabitable. Eagles and other birds of prey nests in the high crags. Water is plentiful - in the summer, when clouds on occasion drift northward from the south, rain can fall in torrents. The Tuaregs pitch their tents on the hillsides, rather in the valley floor. After such rainfall I saw the valleys were covered by a green carpet of plants. The water collects in small lakes or pools. However the soil is too ungenerous to allow the Tuaregs to become anything but a pastoral people.

After resting in Amguid we reached Tamanrasset, capital of Ahaggar Tamanrasset has the Arabized atmosphere. There are wells and date palms. Millet is cultivated in the oasis. One day this will be the forest of oil rigs.

One wonders the origin of these people no one really knows about their history. But, in their long roll down the escarpment of history they have carried their contradiction with them. They are Berbers who wear veils and Berbers who do not; there are Berbers - the majority - inhabiting the mountains who do not understand the language of those Berbers who live in the Sahara desert; there are nomad and semi-nomads and static pastoralists.

Tuaregs have deep-rooted and innate destination of all authority outside that exercised by their own democratic and local organizations, in other simple words, their love of independence, I discovered during my life with them.

The Land of the Kalash

PAKISTAN INTERNATIONAL AIRLINES FLIES TO CHITRAL A FEW times a week from Peshawer, which is a flight we took. This flight is subject to the weather. If the weather in Chitral Valley is bad, one cannot fly out and by road it is 12 hours or more sometimes.

Chitral Valley is the least develop corner of northern Pakistan, and lies between Hindu Kush to the north and west and the mountains of Hindu Raj to the east. Beyond Hindu Kush lies Afghanistan. Through this area passed the Aryans, Alexander The Great, Chingiz Khan, and others who invaded India from the west.

After arriving in Chitral, we checked into the Mountain Inn which is walking distance from the main bazar. The Mountain Inn did not have electricity and only cold running water which is pumped from the well by a small diesel engine. The room has a very nice view of the mountains all around as the Inn is located on a hill.

My wife Susan and myself are mainly interested in visiting a very unique people called Kalash. Kalash means black, because they wear black clothes. They live in Kalash Valley, south of Chitral. There are only a few thousand who live in Birir, Bumburet, and Rumbur. They are pagans and according to legend they are descended from the army of Alexander the Great. Most of the Kalash are white skinned and have fair or dark hair and blue eyes.

They follow their own religion - a mixture of animism, ancestor, and fire worship, and they have their own culture. They make offerings to several gods. Sajigor is the highest deity and is in charge of everything. The other lesser god is Surisan, who protects the animals, Gosheddi, who protects the dairy products, and Praba who protects the fruits and grains.

Their women wear magnificent red and white bead necklaces and superb black headdresses, which flow down their backs and are covered with shells, buttons, and a large red pompom. The only way to go there from Chitral is to rent a jeep and a driver which we did. The jeep was a second world war model. The road traveled south of Chitral parallel to the River Mastuj which becomes later the Kunar River. Our jeep has to stop often due to a leaky radiator and has to be filled with cold water frequently. We traveled to Ayun which is 15 kilometers from Chitral for Bumberet. From here we have to leave the jeep on the road and walked on a footpath climbing parallel to the Bumberet River. It is a hard climb all the way and we have to stop often to rest. We have to walk up a hill about 10 kilometers, about 6 miles to the Bumberet village.

When we arrive in the village, we found their homes are compact, generally windowless structures made from alternate layers of timber and stones or timber and unbacked mud brick. The village was set amongst trees and sited close to the river. The water of the river comes from the melting ice of the high glaciers. It is cold, but refreshing to drink.

After resting a while, we had walnuts to eat, as the village has dozens of walnut trees. Though their economy revolves around sheep and goats, the walnuts are the main source of income. The growing season is very short but they told me that they manage to grow vegetables, maize, cabbages, potatoes, and carrots. They also have plenty of fruits like mulberries, apricots, apples, pears, and plums.

Most Kalash houses are carefully stacked one on top of the other going up the hill. The roof of one house forms the verandah to another house above. The roof is a convenient place to lay out the fruits to dry. The houses are decorated with carvings. Inside the Kalash home I was not allowed to look, but Susan went in. She told me they are dark with floors of packed earth. The cooking is done on an oven hearth and therefore the walls are blackened by the soot.

There are parts of the village reserved for men only. In this area the animals are sacrificed. Goats are sacrificed to gods and ancestors and every man must sacrifice at least once a year. Animal husbandry and sacrifices are male occupations, and the crops are tended by females.

Marriages are arranged during childhood. A fee is paid by the bridegroom to the bride's family. The bride also receives a dowry which is her property. If the wife is unhappy with her marriage, she may elope with her lover and then negotiate with her husband for a divorce.

At death, the body is placed in a carved walnut coffin and left in the cemetery above ground. Wealthy people had wooden effigies made to stand by their coffin.

Kalash have no written language, only a spoken one. It seems it is different than the Chitral language which is Khowar, but Urdu, the national language of Pakistan, is understood everywhere in the country. Kalash language is related to Khowar which is a branch of Indo-

Iranian, which in turn is a the branch of Indo-European languages, commonly known as the Dardic group. The Dardic group is a term applied to the archaic languages of the Hindu Kush.

This valley of Bumberet is at an altitude of between 4875 and 7800 ft above sea level.

One special place in Kalash custom is a Bashali House, which is a house away from the village and generally located on the river. It is a House of Confinement for menstruating and pregnant women. The house is equipped with beds and cooking utensils, and women stay here for around five days. They retire here and rest during menstruation and childbirth. Only women can visit this house - men are not allowed near it or in it. When the woman is finished, she bathes and changes her clothes and return to the village.

I was told when I returned to Chitral that in Birir valley, they hold a festival called Phoo Festival. A Shaman organizes this festival to keep the Kalash population growing. All the shepherds traditionally spend the spring and summer away from the village in high mountain pastures, strengthening their manhood and distinguishing themselves against other men in feats of physical prowess. On the last day of the festival, when all of the village women are dancing, they are allowed by custom to pick as many women as they can satisfy in hopes that these women will be impregnated. Any woman, whether she is married, single, virgin or otherwise can be chosen and thereby truly honored. A child born of such a union is also especially honored, as is the rest of the family, including the husband.

In this festival which lasts for a few days every year, they all put on new clothes, eat special food, and dance around the bonfire with the beating of the drums and singing by the women.

When we finished here, we walked back down hill to the main road and returned to the Mountain Inn in Chitral. On a clear day, we could see against the blue sky Mount Tirch Mir, which is 24,563 ft high in the Hindu Kush mountain range. I remember the last night in Mountain Inn. After sunset, the room boy lit our lanterns for night use in the room, and as a habit when I went into the room I checked to see if any crawly insect was in or around the bed. As I pulled my wife's bed, there on the wall side of the bed sheet was a large scorpion sitting, which had to be killed. I have learned that when I am traveling in remote areas anywhere in the world, I check my bed, shoes, and clothes before I use them. I have found scorpions in shoes or on hanging clothes, snakes in closets or under the bed.

In spite of such problems, traveling in especially remote areas has its own fascination. There are brief intervals, however, in which peace and tranquillity make such travel worthwhile - such intervals I have experienced in Northern Pakistan as well as in Africa, Central Asia, South America and Central America.

The Land Of The Himalaya

ONG AGO BALTISTAN AND LADAKH IN NORTHERN INDIA has always haunted the travelers imagination because of its sheer inaccessibility. Both situated in remote parts of the Himalayas high altitude regions. Now Ladakh which has now become part of Kashmire is under occupation of Indian Army along with Kashmire. I had opportunity to visit these areas before the partition of India while it was still in the British Empire of India.

Now Baltistan is in Pakistan and Ladakh is in India and part of it is under China. I used Mule tracks via Zoji-La Pass to Dras - Kargil & Leh and returned route via to Skardu. This whole area lies between Zanskar Range and Ladakh Range and Karakoram Range all part of the Himalaya Mountains, the world highest mountains.

The population of Baltistan and Ladakh consists of Mons, Dards, and the Tibetans. The Mons are a pastoral community from south of the Himalayas who converted to Buddhism from Hinduism, and mostly they are carpenters, blacksmith, and musicians. The Dards are peasants of Indo-European stock and settled in Dras and Hanu. In Dras, bordering Baltistan converted to Islam, like the entire Baltistan is a Muslim area. There are living tradition of central Tibetan-Buddhism and Islam, as well as Afghan, Turkish and Hindu.

This land has the fascinating fusion of ancient religions, centuries of history and stormy political events. Long ago Ladakh was ruled by Tibetean Rulers and later Balistan Rulers and lastly by Hindus and British. The old Caravan routes used by camels, horses and donkeys when I visited. Now, buses, jeeps and airplanes fly in and out to Skardu in Baltistan and to Leb in Ladakh.

In the name of modernization, now Ladakh is exploited by India under the all present Indian Army in their country. While traveling in this part of the World I noticed that there is a sense of dramatic contrast here and heightened color, tint of yellow, gold, brown and green hills. Small hamlets with small fields break the pattern of the mountain wilderness and snow covered peaks where snow never melts. From a distance it is difficult to distinguish a village from a rocky background: all seem part of a marvelous unity.

You are traveling in a narrow valley between the mountains with dozens of snow covered peaks and just a few miles away you could stumble upon rich meadows with lush grass for the mules to munch, sheep grazing and also yaks being milked and little children playing in this pastoral setting. If you are lucky, which I was I saw the rare Ibex in the distant hillside.

Rivers are born in high altitudes by melting snow that increases the volume of water cascading down the gorge into the plat land. The sound of rapid moving water which is to me is like a song of joy as it dances down from its icy heights.

River Indus flows this land and helps to fill the irrigating channels in the plat villages. Closer to Leh the mountains hem you again, until a sudden dip in the ridge ahead give you your first view of the capital. Prayer flags strung together sweeps upwards to the rocky eminence of Palace Hill crowned by the fort and temple of Namgyal Tsemo. Flat-roofed white-washed houses could be seen all over this area. Leh is the capital of Ladakh.

Further up the track is Leh Bazar. The open market of the Bazar once awaited customers from Tibet, China, India, and as far as Central Asia and Persia The town of Leh is enclosed by a low wall, with square towers approachable through narrow dirt lanes.

The Ladakhi male's dress is like Tibetan coat with colorful facing and a cummerbund. The women wear a beautifully styled dress gathered at the waist and line with brocade. It is worn with colorful pyjamas. On special festive occasions women were a unique head-dress shaped like a cobra-hood from red felt onto which uncut turquoise stones are stitched in rows. Two curved flaps covered with lambs wool extend over the ears. All the women in this part of the World have always enjoyed on festival occasion, wearing and displaying jewelry-silver necklaces, amulets and rings.

Climb any height around Leh and you cannot fail to notice the contrast of stony desert and luxuriant fields, patches of green enclosed by stone walls in the midst of which flat-roofed houses in the summer season. Sometimes the village hangs at the very edge of a cliff, sometime it lies scattered across a valley. Below Leh flows the Indus, the river is only part of the way on its 1,600 kilometer journey to the Arabian Sea.

The Indus region is a veritable garden where summer stretches from June to October permitting double-cropping and autumn brings its harvest of fruit.

The length and severity of winter with heavy snowfall brings misery.

At low altitudes the main crop is wheat and important ingredient of the local bread and other staple is Sattu the naked barley which grows without husk. Rice is imported and eaten on special occasions. The main fruits are apricots, grapes, and melon grown only in the summer. Trees, animal and man accommodate and adopt to an environment that is known to be benevolent to those who observe its laws. In the Asiatic tradition, agricultural operations depend heavily on livestock and in this region too every rural family will try and buy a Dzo (a hybrid of a male yak and a cow) and several cows. The Ladakhi culture has a great influence of Tibetan Buddhism. Ladakh is divided into clearly defined cultural zones. West of Mulbekh lies the Islamic center of Kargil and east of Mulbekh is the Buddhist citadel. Kargil has mosques just like Kashmire mosques and the life in many ways is similar to Kashmire where the majority of people are Muslims - Leh has monasteries and murals and masterpieces in metal-work and icons.

Ladakh crafts reflect the splendor of nature's tints, using rust-red, ochre and umber from the fossil-rich rocks, amethyst, lapis and turquoise to embellish these tones and the gold of sunrise or the smoky purple of the twilight to reflect the life giving forces. Spinning and weaving of wool, wood carving and Thang-Ka painting have been the favored crafts.

As the festival horns and drums and masks called the faithful Buddhist to attention. Ladakhi religious dance remains within the Tibetan tradition. No social event or activity - sowing or harvesting, a wedding or a festival - is complete without music. Ladakhis find it difficult to articulate and define their folk culture. Since it is so much a part of their daily life, they have not tried to seek its sources, study its forms, analyze its contents or record its historic development.

I have been fortunate to observe the Gompa festival which is solemn and dignified. Festival ceremonies begin with the unfurling of the great Thang-Ka. The Rinpoche or the Chief Lama enters and is ceremonially seated. The Lamas are summoned by the beat of the drums. Each enters with his hands raised above his head, then prostrates himself before the Chief Lama then they sit in rows from east to west in the courtyard and then the Chief Lama begins the ceremonies by recitation from sacred Buddhist texts. This is followed by instrumental music which includes drums, horns, symbols, trumpets, and bells. The copper trumpets are about eight to then feet long. Recitation, chants and music alternate with dances. The dancers wear paper-mache masks representing ferocious beings. Mahakalis and Dakinis and the symbolic movements of the dancers is obviously related to exorcising evil spirits.

Outside the ceremonies a bazar is set up where tea, Chang (barley wine) and other food is on sale. Marriages are also an occasion of general festivity. Marriage is generally initiated by the groom's family with an offering of a Chang to the bride. Often the go-between is a lama and a date is fixed. In towns the family share the cost incurred, but in the villages the community bears the major expenditure of the marriage feast. Each family contributes something, wheat, barley, sugar, apricots, butter, tea, or milk. Muslim weddings are similar, except that in place of Chang the tea is served.

Polo is an integral part of summer activities, played anywhere and with any number of players, depend on the size of the level ground and number of players available. The polo is originally started in Baltistan which was copied and developed in west by British. The Ladakhi Polo is Balti style, where the player is allowed to handle the ball and throe it into the goal. The Chukkers of the games are divided into nine goals and the only foul is to cut across the path of another horseman. Skill is defined by a flamboyant style of the horsemanship and a steady eye. In Kargil the standard of archery is much higher than Leh area.

The Ladakhi diet is poor in quality and quantity, because it is dependent on the seasons and the scarce availability of different ingredients. But it is well suited to the climate and environment for each dish contains the ingredients which are vital to compensate for the dryness and cold. Tsampa which is parched barley flour mixed into a gruel is eaten with buttered tea or Chang to combat the vigor of the climate. Well to do people vary their diet with Thug-Kpas which is made like a soup consisting of meat, vegetables and small flat noodles. These noodles are made of wheat and gram flour.

Another popular dish is Skyu which is fried wheat-flour dumpling, mixed with meat, potatoes and turnips. Another Tibetan delicacy is Mok-Mok which is steam-cooked meat dumplings eaten with Gya-Tuk, chinese style egg noodles. Ladakhi bread is make of flour of the wheat similar to Pakistani Paratha but it is thick between the two griddles. I never liked their tea with floating Yak's butter.

Ladakhi Buddhist have lived peacefully with Kargili Muslims contrary to the Hindus of India who constantly tried to provoke their 100 million Muslim minority in their beliefs and daily life. Now, Ladakhi like Kashmire is completely occupied by Indian Army which rules majority population of Muslims in Kashmire with iron hand.

India's bad relation with China has closed the Silk Road to Yarkand and a little trade with India through Zaji-La Pass or to Baltistan in Pakistan and also no communications with Aksai-Chin in Tibet now under China. The old peaceful country is in turmoil because of the lack to trade and the outside world does not know much about it or care about it. Peace and survival of life on earth as we know are threatened by human political greed. The lack of respect to the minority cultures who are like us earth's human descendants, the future generations who will inherit a vastly degraded planet if the world peace does not become a reality in our time.

The Land Of The Lacandes

HE OBJECTIVE OF THE LACANDONES EXPEDITION WAS to study and record the Lacandon Indians of the State of Chiapas, their Maya heritage, and their admixture of present day culture of Modern Mexican.

By living with the Lacandones we had to determine their daily life, arts and crafts, agriculture methods, mythology, religion, costume, customs and habits. The most important aspect of the study was to determine what the few Lacandones left still possessed from their Maya ancestors in pure form.

The secondary aspect of the study was to ascertain the influence of modern civilization in their daily life and what the future holds for them. In simplifying the comparative study of the Lacandones it is important to study Maya culture of the past and then relate the Lacondones of today, The result will be what the Lacandones have lost of the magnificent past - their classic culture. They are now at the verge of disappearing all together and will join the roll of the "Vanishing Cultures of the World."

Lacanha tribes live about 7000 ft in the Southern Sierra Madre on the border of Mexico and Guatemala. They live in the remote mountain top, cut off from any town nearby. The nearest town is two days walk on the mountain foot path. There is no road to reach them. The only way to reach them is by walking, or by hiring a single engine plane to land on a grass strip just barely long enough to land on the mountain top. On the mountain top there are about a dozen grass huts, where the Lacandones live.

After arriving by bus from Palenque our base camp was in a small tour called Toneseque. From here we left most of our heavy baggage in a small hotel and prepared backpacks to carry with us to Lacanha. We discovered that we could rent a single engine plane with and owner-pilot. He was willing to fly us there and come back on a set date to pick us up. The pickup date was subject to the weather and the cloud ceiling in the mountain.

We had to purchase all our supplies in Toneseque as we were told there is nothing available but corn and fresh stream water in Lacandona. The weather was clear so the two of us loaded with our backpacks and left by this small plane at noon. It seems the plane had a hard time to climb to the altitude of 7,000 ft with a full load of three people and our baggage.

After over an hours flight we made a bumpy landing and as soon as we stopped taxing, from no where in this jungle top, came a dozen people with long unruly hair and long white robes surrounded the little plane. These were the descendents of Mayas, who took refuge from Spanish Conquerors. Our pilot had a long discussion about the purpose of our visit and then one man named Arthuro had a volunteer to put us up in his hut. We had our own hammock which we put in his hut. There were two more hammocks, one for his wife and one for himself. This grass hut was all they possessed. It was their living room, dining room, storage and kitchen when it rained. Otherwise, the food was to be cooked outside in the open. For bathing there was a icy cold mountain stream about two feet wide and a foot deep.

The days were cold but pleasant, but the nights were windy and freezing cold. The winds came through the thatched walls of the hut. Our toilet was behind the buses near the stream.

Sooner we settled down at Arthuro's place and the entire village which consisted of about twenty-five people visited us and sat and watched us, until they were tired of looking at us and it got dark and they left. I know only a little spanish and so did Arthuro, that is how our conversation was to be during our stay. After all our provisions of crackers, cheese, coffee, and sugar, which where shared by all the villagers, ran out, our daily diet was tortias cooked hot, bananas, and cold stream water to drink. Our days were spent visiting the families, and sitting and watching their daily routine of life.

Historic Background

PRELITERATE PEOPLE CAN ONLY BE SEEN THROUGH THEIR art. The Maya began somewhere around 2000 BC down to 987 AD. There are no tangible records and no traditions. There is nothing butthe evidence of buildings, sculpture, murals, and pottery. The puzzling aspect is that they developed glyph script language capable of recording events, yet until now nothing is discovered beyond certain calendaric dates. There are many Mayan mysteries still to be solved. They fought few wars, and viewed life from their jungle fastness with Olympian detachment. They were also seafarers along with the Inca, Aztec, Chimu, and Mochica, and used the sea for maritime traffic.

After the fall of Aztecs it took Spaniards from 1527 to 1546 to conquer Yucatan and still the Itzas carried the Maya way of life in El Peten until 1697. Mayan archaeological history began at Palenque. These ruins were discovered by Indians in 1773. Mayan people's sheer will to culture finally conquered nature by raising tall stone temples which loom over the tallest jungle. The monuments remain, the intellectuals disappeared. Very few remains in the pure Maya form in the jungles of Chiapas whom we called Lacandon's. They dress like Maya, speak Mayan, but have with time lost the zest of living. There seems to be few leftover of a defeated nation who where intellectually willed. At the height of Mayan civilization their forefathers were serf, farmers or were in menial employment of the better one's. It is my opinion that for centuries, as the jungle protected and hid the temples and palaces of Maya, it also protected the few pure Mayas in the jungle from outsiders till the advent of the airplane.

Mayan people developed out of the various groups whose common ancestors were those Mesolithic wanderers that century upon century poured across the Bering, a land bridge, once connected Asia with Alaska. Mayan society was organized on kinship bases and they developed from hunting-fishing stage and turned farmers and then eventually became temple builders and myth makers. Perhaps the ancestors of Lacandones were proto-Maya living on hot gulf coast and doubtless inland into the low flat Tehuantepec isthmus and later followed the Rio Usumancinta into the dense jungles and Sierras of Chiapas.

The Mayas were people of wit, passion and interest. Their polychromatic pottery, perhaps the already formed upper classes, a stratified society where inequality is stressed. Archaelogy reveals that population centers, small, compact and self-contained would spring up all over these areas during the long formative period i.e. between 1000 - 300 BC. Trade, language, and common culture rather than political ties held them together as "Mayas".

Whatever the causes, the cities within a wide range of the humid forest were abandoned. What happened to the people? Where did three million people go? Or did they go at all? There was no large scale wars. The cities some of the most impressive monuments built by man anywhere were just left to be enfolded by the tentacles of the jungle flora.

The great influence on highland Mayas was Toltec invasion which they followed the course of the Usumacinta River inland and upward into Guatemalan highlands. This was the time of Maya renaissance, art and architecture flourished anew. Qquetzalcoatl influence bought about the Toltec motifs throughout the region including Puuc and Chinchin Itza. In early 12th century Mayapan became the leading city-state. A century later in a war Cocoms expelled the Toltec. Then came the revenge by Toltec (Itzab) who attacked Mayapan and killed all the Cocoms. After five hundred years the city finally became desolate in 1441 AD. Thus so came the end of Maya by the Spaniards with a final blow by 1546. A civilization of America disappeared in thin air leaving behind magnificent monuments and few Mayas now living in the jungles in a primitive state called Lacandones.

The People

HE MAYAS AVERAGE HEIGHT WAS 5 FT 1 INCH AND HE was robust and strong. They were the most broad-headed people in the world. The Lacandones features closely resembles that of ancient monuments. As soon as the baby was born, his head was artificially flattened by being placed within two tied boards. Mayas believed that this custom was given to then by the gods. It gave them a noble air and helped them better adapt to carry loads tied up on the back and then hanged it by the strap across the forehead. Lacandones have discontinued this practice but they still carry the load in the same fashion.

Ear lobes were pierced for pendants and so was septum of the nose and so the left side of the nose, and when rich you would wear a topaz in their nose. This is also in practice in Asia. Lacandones have abandoned this practice.

The hair was long, black and lustrous, wrapped around the head and braided like a wreath, leaving the greave to hang down behind like "tassels". Facial hair was pulled out by copper tweezers. The Lacandones of today have straight black hair fell loose over their shoulder and male and female have this practice continued.

The tattooing of the bodies by Mayas have also been discontinued by the Lacandones. Maya eyes are dark and lustrous and are typical mongolic. Maya skin color varied from light brown to dark copper. Painting of the face and body was general among men. Black was used by unmarried men, red by warriors, blue by the priests and those to be sacrificed.

The women painted their faces, breasts, arms and shoulders of red colon paint which was a mixture of Achiote and Ix Tahte the liquid amber resin. The paint has a certain perfume also it protected them against sun rays and insects. Which I found all primatives of tropical forests except pygmies use. For dress they use a long hand woven cloth with holes for the arm and the neck which was called by Mayas as Kub but Lacandones today called the same cloth Achanook as drawn in fig. 1.

Women married young. On average, they had seven children. They were good nurses because the constant grnding of tortillas agitated their breast and as none wore any bra they developed large and loose breasts which supplied ample milk except in the case of under nourished mothers. They wore cotton material in company of other women. The practice of weaving is dying out among Lacandones with the advent of modern civilization and only time they weave is when they have to make a marriage Achnook for bride and bridegroom.

Maya women had no gods of love and the goddess Ix Chel was patroness of pregnancy. Lacondones women have a continuous state of pregnancy and the result is after two or three children she looks old due to hard work, lack of normal comforts, malnutrition, and hostile environment, and the result of this is polygamy.

Lacandones women are generally fat in comparison to their husband for various reasons: diet, lack of exercise, and lack of interest to be attractive. On the contrary, man has to farm, hunt, fish, carry firewood, do repair and construction when required, keep him in trim position. Secondly he receives a larger portion of meat and other choice food and the balance of the left over is shared by the woman and the children. Woman's diet has excessive starch and less protein.

Many other tribes which I have visited in Africa and Central and South America women do take interest in making themselves attractive to men by making jewelry or painting themselves etc. But, Lacandones women seem to have lost interest in herself and her looks which is quite contrary to her Maya ancestors. It is in my opinion it is a matter of psychological degradation due to lack of festivities and gay functions and those Lacandones who have accepted Prystatarism only celebrate Christmas and Easter and both cases it is just a big dinner and lots of talk. The old Maya functions are prohibited to them when they use the sing and dance and occasionally got drunk and enjoyed the life. Now life is a harsh solemn affair without letting oneself go once a while. The constant fear of sin has been embedded, the drink has been prohibited, gaity has gone and the life is a drab routine day after day. With the gaity gone so has the music, the dancers, and laughter.

Maya Speech

MAYA IS SPOKEN TODAY BY MOST INDIANS OF YUCATAN, Chiapas and Guatemala. The were more than fifteen dialects spoken such as Chontal in centre, Tzeltal, Ixil, Quiche in Guatemala. Maya language is not closely related to any Central American language but there are certain linguistic links between Maya and Mexican on the north coast especially at the great trading centre of Xicalango and with culture of Teotihuacan. When Toltec made large scale penetration in Mayadon they were speaking Maya. The language used in the League of Mayapan was Mayathan, but there were many problems in case of dialects e.g. a person from Yucatan in 7th Century needed an interpreter to talk to Cholti speaking Itza-Maya people of Lake Peter in Guatemala. This shows a great divergent linguistic evolution which took place within Mayadon. The language spoken on the coasts and plains was more polished than in Sierra and Silva simple because of more desire and opportunity to devote time on conversation.

Lacondones language of today shows lack of enough vocabulary and polish. They have fewer verbs than lowland Mayas. Lacandones use simple sentences without a consideration of correct grammar. They use more verbal noun due to weak in verbs. A litral translation of Lacandones would be like this: "His influencing the maize, the death god heaped up death."

In our literary forms this should read: "Much death will be the result, for the death god now rules the growing maize.

Society

AYA SOCIETY WAS COMPOSED OF: ARISTOCRATS AND nobles; priests; farmers and workers. The aristocrats and noblemen were the Maya lords. They were chief administrators of city states, generals of the army. The Mayas were not an empire as the Incas in South America nor they had tribute-gathering organization of Aztecs. They did not have central Mayan organization, no central ruler etc., but there was a common Mayan culture, language, and religion. No Maya nobleman had ever an imperial ambition why? Maya society was like city-states of Greece. Maya society was self-contained and based on household economy and it was a clan society based on the principal that group is more important than individual. The individual is a member of a family first and then of his state. A wrong done to him is a wrong done to his state.

In terrible cities the farmers brought their produce to the priests to make contact with gods, the people knew of course that the priest eats the produce but they expected priests to make contact with the gods. The priests maintains the temples and are themselves maintained by the products and services of the farmers and workers.

High culture must originate with an aristocratic class for only such class has time and energy to create it, a comporation of priests is developed who took the responsibilities as god contacts and to see that the rituals are followed. Among the Maya, each family was assigned a piece of land of four hundred square feet. The land was worked communally. Lacandones have the habit today of helping each other in all their labors. The community helps in harvesting, house building and any such projects. Mayas had exogamous surmane marriage taboo. They always call them sons and daughters by the same name of the father and mother. We found Lacandones continue this practice today who do not follow Christianity strictly.

Marriage

NE OF THE STRINGENT TABOOS WAS THAT A MAN COULD not marry a woman having the same surname as himself, but he could marry a woman stremming from his mother's line, even a first cousin. Mayas did not seek wife for themselves but through a female match-maker. Sometimes father arranged marriages between sons and daughters in infancy an old world custom in medieval period. Marriageable age for Maya men was eighteen and fourteen for the girls.

Greeks regarded homosexual love as normal thing but Maya have no evidence to show they indulge in such practices but they did entertain public women (Guatepol) in their homes. The women received cacao beans for their services. Monogamy was practiced among the farmers and workers.

When the young men waited to marry, his father arranged a dowry (Muhul) or the marriage service, the priest arranged a lucky day by looking his astrological book. The mother-in-law then wove new garments for the bride and bridegroom and the bride's father prepared the house for the ceremony and feast.

In primative society virginity is not generally highly valued. A Maya girl could not be overzealous about a mere hymen. Marriage for Mayas was matrilocal: the son went to the father-in-law's house and worked for him for about five years. As such Maya marriage was funda-mentally permanent.

Like Greeks, marriage could be repudiated if there were no children. When a couple was divorced the younger children stayed with the mother. The older son went to the father, but the daughters always remained with their mother. Divorce was common. The widowed husband could not marry again for a year after his wife's death.

Lacandones follow all the old Maya customs including polygamy except there are no priests and no temples left and the date to marry is now decided with the consultation of the Chief of the village. The Chief of "Lacanda" had total ten wives but three are alive and living with him and the other seven have died leaving scores of children and grandchildren. Those Lacandones who are Christians still practice polygamy. Among Lacandones the bridegroom still works for his father-in-law and joins his family and shares all the hunt and harvest but live in a separate hut (Nah).

The Housing

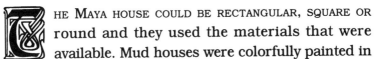 HE MAYA HOUSE COULD BE RECTANGULAR, SQUARE OR round and they used the materials that were available. Mud houses were colorfully painted in the lowland and thatched with palm leaves. Lacandones of today built the house walls of OH and roof covered with palm leaves. The interior of a Maya house was divided by a wall. One part became the kitchen and the other sleeping quarter. Today Lacondones have a day hut and a night one. The day hut has no walls and open from all sides with low palm thatched roof. This hut is generally occupied all the day long and consists of a few hand woven hammocks, kitchen area and hand in hand woven bags the food products are also one can see the bags belonging to their ancestors hanging which may consists of feathers of parrots, Toocan beaks, old animal skulls, or bones etc.

In the night hut it has walls made of OH a bamboo life wood and thatched palm roof. Here, a bed is made of small sapling tied together with hand made ropes from the bark of the trees. The average height of the bed from the floor is 2'6". The bed is covered with a layer of bark of the trees. There is a wooden door in the hut but no windows. In old Maya custom people entered the house with permission, but we observed with Lacandones that there house is open to all at all hours of the day and there is complete lack of privacy. Even early hours of night people walk in and out as they please even if the owner of the house is lying in the bed.

Maya gave names to the various parts of the house as such, the beams were called "the road of the rat", the door "the mouth of the house" and the roof posts "the legs of the house". The Mayas buried their dead under the mud floor of their hut and when all the floor got filled they moved out and the place became a sacred plot. Lacandones have continued this practice.

Arts & Crafts

HE SPINDLE WAS A STICK TEN TO TWELVE INCHES IN length with a pottery balance rings three inches from its end. It was spun about in a small ceramic dish. Lacandones also use the spindle except it is all wooden. As cotton was grown as well as it grew in mild form, weaving was one of the main occupations of women. In Lacandones the weaving is now only used on ceremonial occasions.

Dyes were made from vegetables and mineral, black was obtained from carbon, yellow from ripe corn, red came from achiote, brazilwood and red iron oxide. Cochineal (mukay) was obtained from the insects which Maya boys collected on cactus pads. Blue was obtained from blue chromiferous clay. They also made dyes from wild tomatoes, blackberries, and green-black avocado.

The dyes were pounded in stone mortars. Mordant was required to fix the dyes, the Incas used copper, the Maya used urine and at later stage they used alum. Lacandanes used mostly the same ingredients but are more inclined to use vegetables due the environments they live in. They used alum also to preserve leather. All the art of looms has disappeared with war and conquest and only few areas in Guatemala around Lake Attitlan it is still used in villages. It is a backstrap loom.

Art of featherwork which was highly developed has also completely perished. Lacandones use feathers of green parrots and toucans for their arrows and have no decorative use.

Woven grass mats were extensively used by Mayas. Meals were served on mats, they were used as mattresses for beds but in spite of sufficient material available in the jungle, Lacandones do not use any mats at all and this art is also dead.

Basketry was highly developed. They used reeds, grass and vines for making baskets, then they painted them in pretty designs. This is another dead art among Lacandones.

Pottery is a chronological frame upon which to gauge historic perspectives. The Mayas were pottery makers of high quality. They did not use potters wheel. Pottery was done by coiling. Clay molded into long coils, a sort of outsized spaghetti is laid down in successive rings and worked and pressed into a single form with the hand. The pottery was decorated in extensive designs and patterns and made in all sizes and shapes.

From miniature to life-sized idols were fashioned from the clay. The painting on the pottery gave us many details of Maya life, especially the life of the women, which is never indicated in the carvings on the monuments. All the Maya pottery was done by women. Pottery was exclusively done by women all around the world until the introduction of the potter's wheel. The beautiful designs and patterns on pottery and textile were conceived by women.

Mamom (grandmother) pottery (2000-500BC.) is strictly utilitarian. Utensils and naked clay figures.

Chichanel (concealer) pottery (50BC.-300AD.) Superbly painted polychromatic pottery.

On The Road In Hindu Kush - Pakistan

A Lacanha Man

Monkey
Arrow

Tiger
Arrow

"Mono"
arrow

"Tigro"
arrow

TEPEUH:

Spinden Correlation: 668-570 A.D.
Late Classic Period

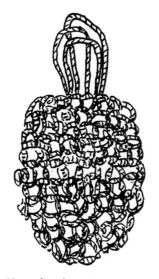

Hand knitted bag

The spindle stick was
rotated on a small pottery
dish. (Illustration from
a Mexican Codex.)
Same type stick is used
today by Lacandóns.

Maya house

Past

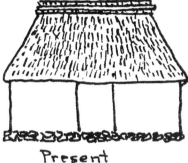

Present
variety

Expedition Base
1971

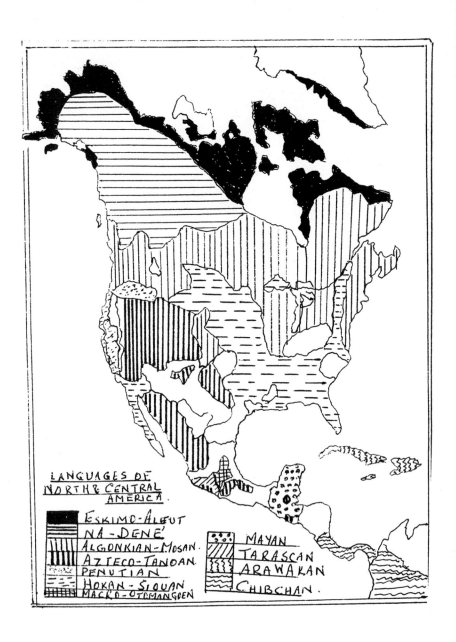

LANGUAGES OF
NORTH & CENTRAL
AMERICA.

ESKIMO-ALEUT
NA-DENE'
ALGONKIAN-MOSAN.
AZTECO-TANOAN.
PENUTIAN
HOKAN-SIOUAN
MACRO-OTOMANGUEN

MAYAN
TARASCAN
ARAWAKAN
CHIBCHAN.

Achanook
used by both sexes

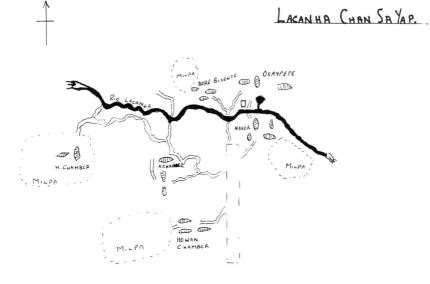

LACANHA CHAN SAYAP.

MAP
OF
CULTURAL DISTRIBUTION OF MEXICO.

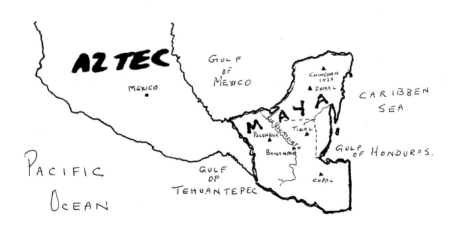

AZTEC

GULF OF MEXICO

MEXICO

CHINCHEN ITZA
UXMAL

CARIBBEN SEA

MAYA

USUMACINTA
PALENQUE
TIKAL

BONANMO

GULF OF HONDURAS.

PACIFIC OCEAN

GULF OF TEHUANTEPEC

COPAL

Tzakol (the builders) pottery (317AD.-650AD.) The period of temple cities. The pottery became more sophisticated and polychromatic. "Thin-orange" a very delicate pottery appeared.

Tepeuh (the conqueror) pottery (650AD.-1000AD.) Here the pottery turns into decorative baroque.

Maya-Toltec the final phase (1000AD.-1500AD.) Pumbate the only glazed pottery appears. Decorated with gods and animals. Toltec motifs, themes from the military orders of the Jaquar and the Eagle appear, as well as variations on the themes of the cult of the pluned serpent.

Tradition and known history are confirmed by the pottery and it by archaeology and this pottery became the "index fossil" of Maya history. Lacandones have no pottery to show their skill and in many ways they are true primitives who have remained isolated during Maya's golden age and have learned nothing in terms of arts and craft of any high order except the basic needs of daily life and these Lacandones are the remnants of the Mayas who took refuge in jungles for known or unknown reasons.

The amazing part is that they have no creative instincts to utilize the facilities and products the environment offers them in such abundance. Their life is harsh appallingly monotonous but they do nothing about it. In the parallel circumstances other primatives whose ancestors were not civilized are far more creative and imaginative in daily life than the Lacandones. It is amazing the predecessors of a high culture could be so degenerates and lack any desire to improve themselves just enough to make daily humdrum of life a little more bareable.

The only art Lacandones have now is making knitted bags, bows and arrows, weaving the hammocks and making bead necklaces. Our host carved out two wooden spoons for Susan. Music and musical instruments are not heard or seen.

Occupations

MAYAS HAD THREE MAIN OCCUPATIONS, AGRICULTURE, hunting and fishing. They did not develop mining to any large extent. They extracted salt from long coastal lagoons around Ekab. Salt was a great trade commodity.

In the interior the cultivated maize fields gave other subsistence crops in addition to corn. Stingless bees were bred in tree hollows. The land abound in honey, used for sweetening and more important for a meadlike intoxicant called Balche.

Cacao, the seed which when dried, toasted and ground is chocolate, was the Maya elixir. It was grown in tropical areas of Tabasco and Chiapas. They also used cacao beans for barter of textile salt and corn.

Maya hunted: Paca, a kind of guinea pig; deer; turkey; rabbit; and iguanas, which tasted life chicken. Turtle and turtle eggs were plentiful. Ain the crocodile tails were a delicacy. The Muscory ducks were raised for plumes as well as for eggs.

One leaches sting rays were killed for their tails, which, armed with razor sharp bones, were used as a saw knife to cut and bleed the body in blood sacrifice by the priests.

The principal food was maize (Chim) from which they made various foods and also drink. In the morning they drank maize mixed with water called Pozole. In the evening they boiled the corn with ash until softened and then husked, after which it was brayed on a stone grinder until reduced to a thick paste from which women prepared tortillas.

In the day when farmers departed for the fields he took with him several apple-sized balls of ground maize wrapped in leaves. Steeped in water and flavored with burning hot chili peppers and this became his lunch.

Meat was not taken daily, because lack of regular supplies. Meats were mostly cooked in the form of stews of deer meat, fish, tapir (Tzimin), armadillos (Zub), manatee (Sea Cow), and turkey. They boiled chayote, a squash-like vegetable which also supplemented their diet. The avocado was cultivated as were papaya and plaintains. Fish were eaten where available. They fished with harpoon-bows and arrow and with nets in the ocean.

Everyone washed their hands before starting the meal and after the meal. Hunting was done by bows and arrows. Trapping was not common and nor was blow guns. Hemp was raised for its fiber, from which they made an infinite number of things: sandals; ropes; twine; bowstrings; fishing line etc. Maya collected a juice of a tropical tree (Ya) a source of our modern chicle, which they used for adhesion. Lacandones still use it by boiling it to a sticky mass.

It was time to return back to our own civilization. We packed and waited for the sound of the single engine plane to circle over the mountain top, but nothing happened and after waiting for a considerable time we unpacked and assumed that something had happened and the pilot could not come to fetch us. The same thing next day we packed again and nothing happened. Now we decided that if he did not come the next day we might consider walking down the mountain which takes two or three days by foot path to reach the valley down and from there walk on flat plains to reach Tonoseque.

Eventually on the third day of waiting we heard the airplane noise and we packed and gave Arthuro and his wife all the stuff, like hammocks, utensils, and money. We thanked them for providing us the board and lodging in their hut and walked to the airstrip and found Carlos, our pilot, there waiting for us. He told us he could not come due to heavy clouds covering the whole mountains for the last two days. We loaded what was left with us and said good-bye to the entire people who came to see us off. When we were ready to take off a man came to the pilot and asked him if he wanted to go to the Tonoseque and the pilot told him the plane is chartered by him, pointing it to me. I asked him why he wanted to go down and how he would come back, and he explained he needed some medicine and he would walk up. It takes three days to climb back on the foot path. I asked the pilot, could we carry an extra load? He answered we can try, he never carried three passengers and their baggage, we may or may not make it. I told him the man seems to be desperate and so let us try it.

The plane after a bumpy run took off and arrived back at Toneseque and after making the final account Carlos took us in his car to Central Hotel which was our base camp and our luggage was stored there. We thanked Carlos after offering him coffee and a snack and went to our room . The first thing Susan did was rush to the bathroom for a hot, hot shower. My turn was next for the hot shower although I had washed up daily in the freezing stream. The experience with living and learning about their life was worth all the hardship we went through. All this time we spent there we were never afraid, we never missed any of our possessions.

From Toneseque we took buses in four stages back to Mexico City where we rested for a few days and met people at the Anthropological Museum. We flew back to Houston to remember the Incredible Journey we just finished.

My wife Susan who is by profession a teacher, changed into a member of an Expedition very successfully and enjoyed it, except for the cold freezing nights in the hammocks on the mountain tops when we both were extremely cold. She sketched all that appears here. We do not know what happened to the lives of those simple people since we left.

Maya Words Used By Lacandones

English	Maya
English	**Maya**
Good Morning	Ba Aa Ka
Good Afternoon	Ti Wa Ya Neche
Good Night	Tari Vaderchi
Good Bye	Beni Ka
Thank You	Ya Yo
Very Good	Na To Ee
Red	Chuk
White	Cuk
Black	Aek
Bean	Burr
Sugar	Cho'Huk
Milk	Gim Ya Kush
Sweet Yellow Potatoes	Pish
Maize	Ner
Fish	Ka Yee
Water	Hah
Turnip Type Vegetable	Chi Kam
Meat	Buk
Plantain	Pa Tam
House	Nah
Man	She Ep
Woman	Esh Keek
Hot	Chaka Key
Cold	Sees
Baby	Oc Ay
Dog	Pek
Head	E Hor
Arm	E Kap

English	Maya
Hand	Utan E Kap
Leg	Utan Vook
Foot	Itani Vook
Hair	E Fool
Eye	In Wich
Nose	In Ee
Marriage	Ean Rak
Death	Keemi
Sun	Ek Hum
Moon	Eka Nah
Night	Aka Beer
Star	Sap
Father	In Teet
Mother	Ina
Brother	E We Sing
Sister	En Keek
Village	En Ka Har
Rain	Ku Ta Ha
Long Dress	Acha Nok
Bamboo Type Wood	Oh
A Type Of Guinea Pig	Pas Winti
Kayom	Ceramic Drum

Expedition Base was Lakanha but it is called E Ka Har Chan Sa Yap and/or Lakanha Chan Sa Yap by the Lancandones.